A Jewel
in His Crown
Journal

REDISCOVERING YOUR VALUE
AS A WOMAN OF EXCELLENCE

PRISCILLA SHIRER

MOODY PUBLISHERS

CHICAGO

All Scripture quotations are taken from the *New American Standard Bible®*. Copyright © 1960, 1962, 1963, 1968, 1971, 1972, 1973, 1975, 1977, 1995 by The Lockman Foundation. Used by permission.

Quotations taken from *A Jewel in His Crown* by Priscilla Shirer (Moody Publishers, 1999).

Cover photo: © 2003 Rosemary Weller/Stone

ISBN: 0-8024-4094-0

1 3 5 7 9 10 8 6 4 2

Printed in the United States of America

For my husband

Your encouragement reminds me that I am cherished.

Your covering reminds me that I am protected.

Your friendship reminds me that I am supported.

Your prayers remind me that I am not alone.

And most importantly,

your continued love reminds me that I am indeed a jewel in His crown.

CONTENTS

A NOTE TO YOU

Jackson, my eight-month-old son, is upstairs crying. (I hope his dad goes to get him.) I'm staring at a huge load of laundry sitting across the room, waiting to be folded. (Maybe my mother-in-law will pop over and take care of it.) A never-ending parade of dirty dishes is in the sink waiting to be washed, and am I supposed to be cooking dinner tonight? There is so much to do, but right now I am so excited about this Bible study that I had to take a moment to write a short note to you before you begin!

Since I first wrote *A Jewel in His Crown* in 1999, the Lord has been teaching me more and more about what it means to be His daughter, a jewel in the King's crown. This journal is meant to help you interact with these truths in a deeper, more personal way, too. I have taken a step back and have worked through this journal just as I hope you will do. It has challenged me to go deeper, study harder, and know Him more. It has changed the way I have chosen to be a woman, wife, and mother. I hope that it will be a blessing to you as well, and I am honored to share in this journey with you.

Don't feel the need to rush through this. Take your time. You do not have to complete this journal in a certain number of days or within a particular time period. It is intended for your spiritual growth, to encourage your personal time with God, and to remind you of your worth in Him. Do this study the same way you would drink a warm cup of your favorite coffee, . . . no quick gulps—just small thoughtful sips! Try to commit about thirty minutes to each study, and you will be able to capture the deep biblical truths tucked away in each section. (Of course you can always give it more time, and I suspect you may want to.)

As much as I would love for you to be able to devote thirty consecutive minutes, I know how hard that can be! In fact, I can tell you right now that the phone will ring, the baby will cry, your girlfriends will invite you to go shopping, your boss will demand overtime, or your husband will come home early and need something to eat. In fact, I want you to know right off the bat that I believe Satan is going to do everything in His power to keep you from giving God thirty consecutive minutes of your day with this devotional. How do I know this? It's true for me, too! My phone literally just rang, and Jackson is still upstairs crying (where's my husband?). So while I understand the reality of distractions, I encourage you to minimize your distractions as much as possible and devote your time and attention to this study. Trust me, you won't want to be interrupted.

This journal was designed to be used along with the book *A Jewel in His Crown*. Although you don't have to have the book to capture the message of this study guide, I'd encourage you to work through the book and the journal at the same time. The journal will reinforce what you are reading in the book and will give you further insights from God's Word. You may choose to work through the journal after you've read the book, though, while the message is still fresh in your mind.

You'll notice that the journal is broken into thirty parts. Within each part are six main sections:

Gem of the Day introduces the key principle for the day's study.

Understanding God's Word encourages you to study and meditate on a particular passage of Scripture.

Applying God's Truth asks personal application questions that will lead you to look deep within yourself for practical answers.

Recording Key Insights encourages you to take note of how God is speaking to you.

Taking Action helps you to determine a specific goal so that you can begin to obey the Lord right away.

Setting the Stone leads you to a time of prayer based on specific verses from Scripture.

At the end of each part you'll find some blank space for journaling. Feel free to answer the "Consider This" questions from the end of each chapter in _A Jewel in His Crown_ in this space, or use this space to record your thoughts and prayers.

I am confident that God will speak to you as you discover your spiritual identity in Him. I get so excited when I think of the freedom you will experience in your life when your true spiritual identity becomes alive in your heart.

I am praying (and I hope that you'll pray, too) that the Lord will open the eyes of your heart to see Him more clearly and that He will open your spiritual ears so that you will hear Him speak through the Holy Spirit. And most importantly, I am praying that when you do see Him and hear His voice, that you will obey Him. It is in obedience to Him that we find true freedom.

Priscilla Shirer

PART I

A JEWEL IN HIS CROWN

Refer to chapter 1 in *A Jewel in His Crown.*

Gem of the Day

*"She is a woman of excellence whose life's goal is to
adorn the crown of her Master" (p. 13).*

1. Consider what you spend most of your time and energy focused on. Careful inspection of this reveals where your true interests lie. Based on how you spend your time, what is your primary life goal? Circle one or write in your own idea.

   Beauty   Marriage

   Educational achievement   Successful career

   Family   Glorifying God

   Financial security   Other _____

Understanding God's Word

2. The psalmist says we are fearfully and wonderfully made. Read the following passage and reflect on what you learn about your worth in God's eyes. "Are not two sparrows sold for a cent? And yet not one of them will fall to the ground apart from your Father. But the very hairs of your head are all numbered. So do not fear; you are more valuable than many sparrows" (Matthew 10:29–31).

_____

_____

_____

*For You formed my inward parts; You wove me in my mother's womb.
I will give thanks to You, for I am fearfully and wonderfully made;
Wonderful are Your works, And my soul knows it very well.
Psalm 139:13–14*

3. Consider one of the brightest jewels in the King's crown—Mary, the mother of Jesus. (Mary's story is recorded in Luke 1:26–38.) What trait or characteristic can you uncover about Mary from her response to the angel in Luke 1:38 that would explain why she may have been the one chosen to bear the Messiah? Do you have that same characteristic?

_____

_____

_____

"God looked down on the earth and saw many women who were potential mothers for Jesus, but after the search was complete, He chose Mary. She was a virtuous woman who loved and cherished both herself and her Lord enough to go through what was undoubtedly the most agonizing experience of her life" (p. 15).

The angel said to her, "Do not be afraid, Mary; for you have found favor with God." Luke 1:30

4. Mary understood how precious she was to God; therefore she accepted His plans for her with great joy. Why is it easier to trust God and obey Him when we are confident that He loves and favors us?

_____

_____

_____

5. God's favor = God's protection, God's sovereignty, God's blessings, God's anointing, and much more! Take some time to think about what God's Word says about your incredible worth. Start by meditating on Psalm 139:1–18. Write out a few of your favorite verses—either from Psalm 139 or elsewhere—in the space below. What do these Scriptures tell you about God's perception of your value?

_____

_____

_____

𝒜PPLYING GOD'S TRUTH

6. Think for a minute about a modern, real-life example of a woman of excellence (preferably someone you know personally). Describe her below. Then compare your own characteristics with those that make you admire this woman.

_____

_____

_____

7. How would you want others (friends, family, coworkers) to describe you as an example of a woman of excellence?

_____

_____

_____

8. How comfortable are you with thinking of yourself as a precious, priceless jewel in the King's crown? Check one. Why?

☐ very comfortable   ☐ somewhat comfortable   ☐ uncomfortable

_____

_____

_____

9. Thinking of ourselves as royalty may take some getting used to! This is especially true when our background, past relationships, family, etc., may have given us conflicting messages. Make a list of people or situations that have influenced your perception of yourself. Compare those influences with what Scripture says about your worth to God.

_____

_____

_____

RECORDING KEY INSIGHTS

10. What verses or insights from today's study were particularly significant to you? Write them below and journal about what they mean to you.

_____

_____

_____

TAKING ACTION

11. What will you do differently as a result of today's study?

_____

_____

_____

SETTING THE STONE

Allow these verses to inspire your prayerful response to God today:

☐ *Psalm 103:11*—That I will know his measureless love for me.

☐ *Jeremiah 1:5–10*—That I will do what God has appointed me to do with confidence, knowing He loves me.

☐ *Luke 1:28*—That I will recognize myself as God's favored one.

Journal notes

Journal notes

PART 2

BEAUTY FROM THE INSIDE OUT

Refer to chapter 1 in *A Jewel in His Crown*.

*G*EM OF THE DAY

*"We can't shine on the outside unless God's power is at work on the inside.
No matter how much work we put into the outside, it will be worthless unless we
are plugged into the true power source of our beauty. All the makeup in the
world will not matter when the inside is a mess" (p. 26).*

1. Approximately how many minutes or hours per day do you spend beautifying or taking care of yourself physically? _____ Approximately how many minutes or hours per day do you spend beautifying or taking care of yourself spiritually? _____ What does this simple comparison reveal about your priorities?

_____

_____

_____

*U*NDERSTANDING GOD'S WORD

*"If you are royalty, you don't have to flaunt it—people will just know. They will know
because of the air that you carry, not because of the stuff that you carry. . . . A diamond
doesn't have to be flashy or flamboyant to be breathtakingly beautiful" (p. 22).*

*Your adornment
must not be merely
external—braiding
the hair, and wear-
ing gold jewelry, or
putting on dresses;
but let it be the
hidden person of
the heart, with the
imperishable qual-
ity of a gentle and
quiet spirit, which
is precious in the
sight of God.
1 Peter 3:3–4*

2. Read 1 Peter 3:3–4. With what must you adorn your inner self in order to be precious in the sight of God? What are some practical ways you can do this?

_____

_____

_____

3. Read 1 Samuel 16:7 and Proverbs 31:30. In what ways do you depend on your external appearance to find favor with others or with God?

_____

_____

_____

4. Let's look at the example of another virtuous woman, Hannah, in 1 Samuel 1:1–28. We have no record of Hannah's outward appearance. What insight can you glean from this passage about her heart?

Charm is deceitful and beauty is vain, But a woman who fears the Lord, she shall be praised.
Proverbs 31:30

_____

_____

_____

"If Hannah had been outside of the will of God, she would not have experienced all the joy and blessing that God intended for her. If she had given birth to Samuel any earlier than at the intended time, it would have been the wrong time. God had a plan that exceeded Hannah's deepest desire. He was interested in what her son would do for the entire nation of Israel" (p. 17).

5. Reflect on how Hannah expressed her devotion to God's desires in 1 Samuel 1:10–11. What is the deepest desire of your heart right now? Try putting it into words below.

_____

_____

_____

6. Have you shared this with the Lord? If so, how do you believe He has responded?

$\mathcal{A}$PPLYING GOD'S TRUTH

7. We often worry about our *circumstances,* what's going on outside of us. God is more concerned with our *character,* what's happening inside us. As He did with Hannah, God uses our external circumstances to mold our character. How is God working on the person you are becoming as you wait for the fulfillment of your heart's deepest desires? How does this bring Him glory?

---

8. What may be holding you back from letting Him have His way in your life? Prayerfully journal your confession and desire to repent regarding what God reveals to you.

$\mathcal{R}$ECORDING KEY INSIGHTS

9. What verses or insights from today's study were particularly significant to you? Write them below and journal about what they mean to you.

*T*AKING ACTION

10. What will you do differently as a result of today's study?

_____

_____

_____

SETTING THE STONE

Allow these verses to inspire your prayerful response to God today:

☐ *Psalm 19:14*—That my heart's deepest desires will please God in all respects.

☐ *Matthew 23:26*—That I will prioritize spiritual beauty above physical beauty.

☐ *Ephesians 3:20*—That I will remember He is able to do more with me than I can imagine.

Journal notes

Journal notes

PART 3

DIAMONDS IN THE ROUGH

Refer to chapter 1 in *A Jewel in His Crown*.

*G*EM OF THE DAY

*"It is time for us to see ourselves as God Almighty sees us.
Time to stop allowing others to dictate our value and worth.
Time for us to take off the masks that disguise the truth
about ourselves and to get real with God"* (p. 27).

1. What masks do you wear that hide the real you from other people? From God?

_____

_____

_____

2. What one thing would you most like to change about yourself? Try to be realistic and choose something nonphysical and within your control (your temperament, your attitude, etc.). Why?

_____

_____

_____

3. At times you may try to hide the real you behind a mask, but God sees through that and desires to change you—and in other ways than you might choose. His desire is to conform you to the image of His Son. What do you think *God* would most like to change about you?

_____

_____

_____

*U*NDERSTANDING GOD'S WORD

4. Meditate on 1 Corinthians 13:4–8 by substituting "Jesus" for the word "love" (JESUS is patient, JESUS is kind and is not jealous, etc.). Write down what this tells you about Jesus' character.

_____

_____

_____

5. In which of these areas do you most need to conform to Jesus' likeness? Mark the two or three that you struggle with most.

Impatience	Rudeness
Meanness	Self-centeredness
Envy	Short-temperedness
Pride	Unforgiveness

6. Read Philippians 2:5–8 for more evidence of Jesus' character. Record examples of His specific actions and attitudes.

_____

_____

_____

7. Realizing that the goal of our spiritual growth is to be more like Jesus, complete the following statements.

Conforming to the likeness of Jesus means I will . . .

_____

Conforming to the likeness of Jesus means I will not . . .

_____

8. Take some time to reflect on what God's Word says about how and why God wants to change us into the image of His Son, Jesus (see 2 Corinthians 3:18). Review Scriptures we've studied as well as any others you wish to include here.

_____

_____

_____

*A*PPLYING GOD'S TRUTH

9. If we want to be sparkling jewels in His crown, we must be willing to allow God to polish us. We need Him to constantly change our current disposition. This change means growth. Where would you put yourself on the following scale of spiritual growth?

_____

No desire to grow   *Some desire to grow*   *Strong desire to grow*

10. Describe how you have been growing spiritually in the following areas in the last six months.

Finances

_____

Relationships

_____

Studying God's Word

_____

Prayer

_____

Seeking Christian fellowship

_____

Serving others

_____

Other

_____

But we all, with unveiled face, beholding as in a mirror the glory of the Lord, are being transformed into the same image from glory to glory, just as from the Lord, the Spirit.
2 Corinthians 3:18

11. Which of these areas would you like to target for spiritual growth in the next six months?

_____

_____

_____

*R*ECORDING KEY INSIGHTS

12. What verses or insights from today's study were particularly significant to you? Write them below and journal about what they mean to you.

_____

_____

_____

*T*AKING ACTION

13. What will you do differently as a result of today's study?

_____

_____

_____

SETTING THE STONE

Allow these verses to inspire your prayerful response to God today:

☐ *Psalm 130:4*—That I will seek and find forgiveness where I have failed Him.

☐ *2 Corinthians 3:18*—That I will rejoice because I can be more like Jesus today than I was yesterday.

☐ *Philippians 1:6*—For God to continue to perfect the work He has begun in me.

Journal notes

Journal notes

PART 4

IDENTIFYING INFLUENCES

Refer to chapter 2 in *A Jewel in His Crown*.

*G*EM OF THE DAY

"Creators of TV commercials and print ads want to convince women like you and me that if we buy what they are selling, we will [have a better life. . . . However, in doing so] we may have to compromise what we really want for what somebody else wants us to have" (p. 31).

1. We often care so much about what others think of us. In what ways do you seek the approval of others?

   _____

   _____

   _____

*U*NDERSTANDING GOD'S WORD

2. Look at the kinds of things Philippians 4:8 says should fill our minds. What specific things come to mind that would fit this description?

   _____

   _____

   _____

Finally, brethren, whatever is true, whatever is honorable, whatever is right, whatever is pure, whatever is lovely, whatever is of good repute, if there is any excellence and if anything worthy of praise, dwell on these things.
Philippians 4:8

"You and I often allow Satan to get the best of us and to fill our minds with things that are untrue about our standing with Christ" (p. 33).

3.   Read Galatians 4:7. How did you go from being a pauper to a princess?

_____

_____

_____

4.   You may be familiar with the prodigal son's story (see Luke 15:11–24). Talk about self-esteem issues—the beloved son of a wealthy man was sharing a pig's pen! In what specific ways are you living in a spiritual "pig pen" and forfeiting your position as a royal princess in Christ?

_____

_____

_____

5.   What types of negative thoughts about yourself have kept you from your true potential in Him?

_____

_____

_____

"Hold up your head and don't forget the way God sees you. It doesn't matter what circumstances you are up against. Nothing and no one should cause you to drop your eyes to the floor in defeat, for He is 'the One who lifts [your] head' (Psalm 3:3). You are royalty because of your birthright in Christ. No matter what anybody else thinks, you are part of the King's royal court. Remember who you are!" (p. 33).

6.   Take some time to reflect on what God's Word says about the importance of gaining our self-esteem from what God thinks of us, not what others think. Review Scriptures we've studied as well as any others you wish to include here (see Genesis 1:26–27 and 1 Corinthians 6:19–20 for further study).

_____

_____

_____

$\mathcal{A}$PPLYING GOD'S TRUTH

7. Consider all the influences that shape the way you see yourself, including your physical appearance, your job, your status in your community or at church, your family, the media, etc. Describe the effects—both positive and negative—that these influences are currently having on your self-image.

_____

_____

_____

8. If we are chosen to be royalty, we'd better start acting like it! Based on your understanding of what God's Word says about you, what attitude or behavior unbecoming of a princess are you currently displaying? Be honest here—no one will read this but you. And God already knows the answer!

_____

_____

_____

$\mathcal{R}$ECORDING KEY INSIGHTS

9. What verses or insights from today's study were particularly significant to you? Write them below and journal about what they mean to you.

_____

_____

_____

*T*AKING ACTION

10. What will you do differently as a result of today's study?

_____

_____

_____

SETTING THE STONE

Allow these verses to inspire your prayerful response to God today:

☐ **Psalm 139:17–18**—For God's many precious thoughts about me to bring a smile to my face today.

☐ **Proverbs 29:25**—That I will not fall into the snare of fearing what others think of me.

☐ **Romans 12:2**—That I will be transformed as I renew my mind.

☐ **Galatians 3:29**—That I will remember I belong to Christ and am heir to His promises.

Journal notes

Journal notes

PART 5

THE MAKING OF A PEARL

Refer to chapter 2 in *A Jewel in His Crown*.

*G*EM OF THE DAY

"Our task when uncomfortable circumstances invade our lives is to wrap ourselves in the Word of God. It is filled with a substance that will change us forever and make us into the pearls that we were created to be" (p. 45).

1. List the uncomfortable situations you're currently facing in life.

   _____

   _____

   _____

2. Let's face it; we prefer that things in life stay easy. Why do you think people are generally so resistant to any form of challenge? In what ways are you being resistant to your challenges?

   _____

   _____

   _____

*U*NDERSTANDING GOD'S WORD

3. Read Romans 5:3–5. Underline all the positive results of tribulation you can find in this passage. Choose one or two, and reflect on their importance in your life.

   _____

   _____

   _____

And not only this, but we also exult in our tribulations, knowing that tribulation brings about perseverance; and perseverance, proven character; and proven character, hope; and hope does not disappoint, because the love of God has been poured out within our hearts through the Holy Spirit who was given to us.
Romans 5:3–5

4. What changes do you suspect God may be trying to make in your character through the challenges you're facing?

_____

_____

_____

5. In the Bible there are many examples of God's bringing something beautiful from trouble or tragedy. Consider the stories of Moses, Joseph, Job, Esther, or Ruth. What positive results came out of the trials in each of these people's lives?

_____

_____

_____

6. Paraphrase your understanding of Romans 8:28.

_____

_____

And we know that God causes all things to work together for good to those who love God, to those who are called according to His purpose.
Romans 8:28

7. Meditate on Jeremiah 29:11. How does this verse give you a sense of hope, even in disappointing or painful circumstances?

_____

_____

_____

8. Take some time to reflect on what God's Word says about the plans He has in store for you. Review Scriptures we've studied as well as any others you wish to include here.

_____

_____

_____

*A*PPLYING GOD'S TRUTH

"During an oyster's life, a foreign substance of some sort may get caught inside the creature's shell. . . . This substance can be as small as a grain of sand, but when it gets trapped, the unexplainable happens. The oyster secretes a thin sheet of a substance called nacre *that encloses the foreign object. Inside this thin sheet, the foreign object begins to change and become reshaped until it is no longer an insignificant grain of sand but a beautiful, shining, costly pearl" (pp. 44—45).*

9. Remember a time God used "tribulation" to produce a more brilliant sparkle in your Christian character. What was that time like, and what did you learn from it?

   _____

   _____

   _____

10. In what ways do you feel trapped right now in your life? Take some time to pray about the situation. Ask God to work His wonders and transform you into a pearl that shines for His glory.

   _____

   _____

   _____

"For I know the plans that I have for you," declares the LORD, "plans for welfare and not for calamity to give you a future and a hope."
Jeremiah 29:11

11. How does the encouragement in Romans 8:28 apply to your current situation?

   _____

   _____

   _____

RECORDING KEY INSIGHTS

12. What verses or insights from today's study were particularly significant to you? Write them below and journal about what they mean to you.

_____

_____

_____

TAKING ACTION

13. What will you do differently as a result of today's study?

_____

_____

_____

SETTING THE STONE

Allow these verses to inspire your prayerful response to God today:

☐ *2 Chronicles 20:15*—That I will realize that God is in control of my circumstances.

☐ *Romans 8:28*—For God to work all things together for my good and for His glory.

☐ *2 Corinthians 1:5–6*—That I will encourage other women in the King's court concerning their own "pearl-making" process.

☐ *2 Peter 1:3*—That God will continue to give me everything I need to do what He wants me to do.

Journal notes

Journal notes

PART 6

ADVANCING TO ROYALTY

Refer to chapter 2 in *A Jewel in His Crown*.

*G*EM OF THE DAY

*"When a woman recognizes all that she is worth, a new awakening occurs in her.
No longer is she held captive by fears, shame, and guilt. She is free to experience
the joy of the Lord and to reach the full potential of all that
He has in store for her" (p. 39).*

1. When we talk about women's liberation, we might think of suffragists or feminists, demanding equal rights for women. In fact, most American women have adopted some feminist ideals and opinions. But what does it mean to be a "liberated woman" in the spiritual sense? How does this differ from how the world views liberation?

And you will know the truth, and the truth will make you free.
John 8:32

_____

_____

*U*NDERSTANDING GOD'S WORD

2. Read John 8:32. Put into your own words the truth of this verse concerning the life God has called you to live.

_____

_____

3. Reflect on the Christian's "declaration of independence" found in Galatians 5:1. Notice what we are told to do as a result of our freedom in Christ. What does it mean to stand firm?

    _____

    _____

    _____

4. Read the following verses. What do they say about who we are in God's eyes? Because of this, how are we to live in this world?

    2 Corinthians 6:17–18 _____

    Galatians 3:26 _____

    Ephesians 1:5 _____

    1 John 3:1–2 _____

It was for free-
dom that Christ
set us free; there-
fore keep stand-
ing firm and do
not be subject
again to a yoke
of slavery.
Galatians 5:1

"*Have you come to understand that you are royalty? As a daughter of the King, you are a princess, with a prestigious position in His royal court. You are a coheir to the riches of Jesus Christ, and His royal blood pulses through your veins*" (p. 46).

5. Read through the quote above slowly and deliberately, digesting each word. Record your heartfelt response to what you have read.

    _____

    _____

    _____

6. Take some time to reflect on what God's Word says about our freedom in Christ as women in the King's court. Review Scriptures we've studied as well as any others you wish to include here. Look again at my life verse, Galatians 5:1, for further insight.

    _____

    _____

    _____

$\mathcal{A}$PPLYING GOD'S TRUTH

7. As representatives of the King we are expected to act like royalty. A holy God is surrounded by holy people in His court. Imagine for a moment that you belong to earthly royalty. You would encounter certain expectations, wouldn't you? What kind of daily schedule would you be expected to keep? Who would you be expected to spend time with? Where would you be expected to go? How would you be expected to dress? How would you be expected to talk?

8. As spiritual royalty, descendants of Jesus, how should your position in His court affect

your daily schedule?

who you spend time with?

where you go?

how you dress?

your lifestyle choices?

But you are A CHOSEN RACE, A royal PRIESTHOOD, A HOLY NATION, A PEOPLE FOR God's OWN POSSESSION, SO that you may proclaim the excellencies of Him who has called you out of darkness into His marvelous light.
1 Peter 2:9

RECORDING KEY INSIGHTS

9.   What verses or insights from today's study were particularly significant to you? Write them below and journal about what they mean to you.

_____

_____

_____

TAKING ACTION

10.   What will you do differently as a result of today's study?

_____

_____

_____

SETTING THE STONE

Allow these verses to inspire your prayerful response to God today:

☐ **Proverbs 31:10**—That God will help me strive for and achieve excellence in everything today.

☐ **Galatians 5:1**—That I will live in freedom and not allow myself to be a slave to sin.

☐ **1 Peter 2:9**—That I will celebrate my potential as a member of God's royal priesthood.

Journal notes

Journal notes

PART 7

POTENTIAL IN CHRIST

Refer to chapter 3 in *A Jewel in His Crown*.

*G*EM OF THE DAY

"Women who forget their royal position create an invisible barrier between themselves and the potential that Christ has called them to reach" (p. 49).

1. Most women carry an idea or dream for their lives from the time they are little girls. What is your secret dream for your life? Where would you be? What would you do? What would you be like? Let your imagination go and describe your dream below.

_____

_____

_____

2. In what ways is your dream different from the reality of your life?

_____

_____

_____

Now to Him who is able to do far more abundantly beyond all that we ask or think, according to the power that works within us . . .
Ephesians 3:20

*U*NDERSTANDING GOD'S WORD

3. Many women feel frustrated and disappointed because the life they've always dreamed of having seems unattainable. They don't have the power to make their own dreams come true. Yet how does *God's* power compare with our human limitations, according to Ephesians 3:20?

_____

_____

_____

4. Not only do we wonder if God could ever change our lives, but we also wonder if God can change *us*. Our failures can cause us to question if we will ever be the godly women we want to be—the women God desires. Perhaps you wonder, *Is God* really *able to change me?* Read Matthew 9:27–30, and reflect on what you learn about the answer to that question.

_____

_____

_____

As Jesus went on from there, two blind men followed Him, crying out, "Have mercy on us, Son of David!" When He entered the house, the blind men came up to Him, and Jesus said to them, "Do you believe that I am able to do this?" They said to Him, "Yes, Lord." Then He touched their eyes, saying, "It shall be done to you according to your faith." And their eyes were opened.

Matthew 9:27–30

5. Read the following verses, and reflect on what you learn about God's power to work within us.

Romans 4:21 _____

2 Corinthians 9:8 _____

2 Timothy 1:12 _____

"When God created woman, He took extra time and attention to make sure that we are the wonderful creatures that He intended us to be. From the very beginning, His special interest in women has been apparent. God carefully 'fashioned' us, and we should be proud to be such a special part of His creation. If the Master of the universe was pleased when He'd finished creating us, why shouldn't we be happy with ourselves?" (p. 49).

6. Read Philippians 2:13. God promises to give you both the desire to achieve your potential in Him and also the ability to do so. List the specific areas of your life in which you are going to have to completely trust in the Lord to achieve your potential in Him.

_____

_____

_____

7.   What role does the Holy Spirit play in helping you reach your spiritual potential? See John 14:26; 16:13; Acts 1:8; and Romans 8:26.

_____

_____

_____

8.   Take some time to reflect on what God's Word says about our potential to be all that God wants us to be. Review Scriptures we've studied as well as any others you wish to include here.

_____

_____

_____

$\mathcal{A}$PPLYING GOD'S TRUTH

In the same way the Spirit also helps us in our weakness. Romans 8:26

9.   The Bible clearly tells us the Christian's ultimate goal in life is to be like Jesus. How would you rate your potential to achieve all that God wants you to be? Why did you choose that answer?

____very limited   ____somewhat limited   ____limitless

_____

_____

_____

10.   God gave us the Holy Spirit to help us bring glory to God by reaching our full potential—conforming to Christ's image. Spend some time now humbly confessing your own inability to reach your potential, and ask for the Spirit's help to reach this goal.

*R*ECORDING KEY INSIGHTS

11. What verses or insights from today's study were particularly significant to you? Write them below and journal about what they mean to you.

_____

_____

_____

*T*AKING ACTION

12. What will you do differently as a result of today's study?

_____

_____

_____

S E T T I N G   T H E   S T O N E

Allow these verses to inspire your prayerful response to God today:

☐ *Jeremiah 29:12–13*—That I will seek God with all my heart.

☐ *John 10:27*—That I will know God's voice.

☐ *Romans 14:4*—That God will enable me to stand and do His will.

☐ *2 Corinthians 3:18*—That God will transform me into Jesus' image.

Journal notes

Journal notes

PART 8

JUST ANOTHER PRETTY FACE?

Refer to chapter 3 in *A Jewel in His Crown*.

*G*EM OF THE DAY

"The world does not need another Heather Locklear or Pamela Anderson Lee.
The world needs you and me, just the way God made us" (p. 52).

1. From movies to magazines to television programs, there is no doubt that our society is obsessed with physical appearance. What aspect of your physical appearance would you most like to change? Why?

    _____

    _____

    _____

*U*NDERSTANDING GOD'S WORD

2. It's natural to notice someone else's beautiful hairstyle or stylish outfit. However, when you start to compare, beware! List the people you compare yourself to. What do they have that you want? Be honest.

    _____

    _____

    _____

3. What does the Bible say about jealousy and comparing our physical appearance with others? Write your thoughts beside each Scripture.

Proverbs 6:34–35 _____

Proverbs 27:4 _____

1 Corinthians 3:3 _____

James 3:16 _____

4. Read Romans 12:1. What do our physical bodies have to do with our spirituality? How does this message from God's Word compare with the message society gives us regarding the purpose of our bodies?

_____

_____

_____

Or do you not know that your body is a temple of the Holy Spirit who is in you, whom you have from God, and that you are not your own? For you have been bought with a price: therefore glorify God in your body.
1 Corinthians 6:19–20

"Taking the time and energy to make your body the best that it can possibly be is time-consuming and difficult. But it is worth the effort you put into it. You shouldn't let this dominate your life, but it is definitely one of the three parts of becoming a well-rounded woman of distinction" (p. 54).

5. According to Genesis 2:22, God fashioned you. He did not make a mistake in creating you just the way you are. It can be easy for us to concentrate so much on what we don't like about our physical bodies that we forget the things we do appreciate about ourselves. List your physical characteristics that you like.

_____

_____

6. Take some time to reflect on what God's Word says about how we should treat our physical bodies. Review Scriptures we've studied as well as any others you wish to include here.

_____

_____

_____

"A healthy body has no eternal value whatsoever, but it is a very important and necessary part of being a woman of distinction. Our bodies are what God uses as tools to carry out His will on earth" (p. 56).

*A*PPLYING GOD'S TRUTH

7. Scripture says your body is not your own to do with as you please. How does this truth affect the respect you have for your body?

---

8. Impressing others shouldn't be our motivation for taking care of our physical bodies. But respecting our bodies in order to honor God is quite another matter. In light of what you've learned in God's Word, what will you change about the way you take care of your body? On what date will you begin to implement these changes?

---

*R*ECORDING KEY INSIGHTS

9. What verses or insights from today's study were particularly significant to you? Write them below and journal about what they mean to you.

*T*AKING ACTION

10. What will you do differently as a result of today's study?

_____

_____

_____

SETTING THE STONE

Allow these verses to inspire your prayerful response to God today:

☐ *Proverbs 4:20–22*—That I will study God's Word, which brings health to my body.

☐ *1 Corinthians 9:27*—That God will help me be disciplined in the way I treat my body.

☐ *2 Corinthians 4:11*—That others will see Jesus because of the way I present myself.

☐ *2 Corinthians 7:1*—That God will show me what contaminates my body and spirit, so that I can turn from those ways.

Journal notes

Journal notes

PART 9

MIND OVER MATTER

Refer to chapter 3 in *A Jewel in His Crown*.

*G*EM OF THE DAY

"Truly smart women are those who continue to build themselves mentally instead of allowing all of that glorious brain tissue to go to waste. God blessed you with it, so why not use it?" (p. 57).

1. Who is the wisest person you know? How has this person's wisdom been apparent to you?

   _____

   _____

   _____

And [Jesus] said to him, "YOU SHALL LOVE THE LORD YOUR GOD WITH ALL YOUR HEART, AND WITH ALL YOUR SOUL, AND WITH ALL YOUR MIND." Matthew 22:37

*U*NDERSTANDING GOD'S WORD

2. What does the Bible teach us about the significance of our minds? Read the following Scriptures and record your thoughts beside each one.

   Job 38:36 _____

   Psalm 16:7 _____

   Proverbs 15:14 _____

   Romans 8:6 _____

"Mind building has nothing to do with high school or college or graduate school, although those things are great. I am talking about a determination to never stop learning" (p. 59).

3.   Read Matthew 22:37. What does it mean to love God with our minds?

_____

_____

_____

4.   God's Word tells us to do everything for the sake of God's glory (see 1 Corinthians 10:31). How can you, a woman of excellence, glorify God using your mind? In the decisions you have to make today?

_____

_____

_____

"Statistics tell us that most people utilize only 10 percent of their mental capacity. What glorious things could we accomplish if we actually begin to gain access to the other 90 percent?" (p. 57).

And do not be conformed to this world, but be transformed by the renewing of your mind, so that you may prove what the will of God is, that which is good and acceptable and perfect.
Romans 12:2

5.   Believers must make a conscious effort to counteract the world's influence on our minds. What things can you do to renew your mind? See Romans 12:2 for insight.

_____

_____

_____

"The virtuous woman in Proverbs 31 not only was a beautiful woman, but she was mentally prepared to make sure that things were done well" (p. 60).

6.   Read the full description of the wise woman found in Proverbs 31. How does she apply her mental energies toward being a woman of excellence?

_____

_____

_____

7. Take some time to reflect on what God's Word says about how we should use our minds. Review Scriptures we've studied as well as any others you wish to include here.

_____

_____

_____

$\mathcal{A}$PPLYING GOD'S TRUTH

8. The Bible says that if we lack wisdom, we should ask God for it (James 1:5). Write out a prayer asking God to show you how you can become a wise woman. Ask Him to show you specific areas where you need godly wisdom and knowledge.

_____

_____

_____

_____

She opens her mouth in wisdom, And the teaching of kindness is on her tongue.
Proverbs 31:26

9. God's Word is clear about the importance of using your mind to His glory. What can you do to become a lifelong learner? Consider your reading habits, your personal study, your exposure to current events, adult-learning courses, or other activities that engage your mind and broaden your thinking.

_____

_____

_____

Recording Key Insights

10. What verses or insights from today's study were particularly significant to you? Write them below and journal about what they mean to you.

_____

_____

_____

Taking Action

11. What will you do differently as a result of today's study?

_____

_____

_____

SETTING THE STONE

Allow these verses to inspire your prayerful response to God today:

☐ **Mark 12:30**—That I will find ways to love God with my mind today.

☐ **Philippians 4:8**—For my mind to dwell on only what is pleasing to God.

☐ **2 Timothy 2:15**—That I will discipline my thinking and expand my mind in order to "present myself approved" to God in every area of my life.

Journal notes

Journal notes

PART 10

FIRST LOVE

Refer to chapter 3 in *A Jewel in His Crown*.

*G*EM OF THE DAY

*"No one can take the place of your God—not your husband, your boyfriend,
your children, or your parents. No matter how awesome our loved ones may be,
we have to learn that there are some things that only a holy God can do" (p. 60).*

1. How is God's love for you different from every other love you've experienced on
   earth?

   _____

   _____

*U*NDERSTANDING GOD'S WORD

2. Do you remember your first love? What things did your love for him make you willing to do? Read about how Jesus wants to remain our first love throughout our lives
   in Revelation 2:4. Reflect on what it means to have Jesus as your "first love."

   _____

   _____

3. God is a jealous lover. He doesn't want to share your primary affection with anyone
   or anything else. Study the following Scriptures and journal what you learn about
   God's jealous love for you.

   Exodus 20:5 _____

   Deuteronomy 4:24 _____

Psalm 79:5 _____

Jeremiah 31:3 _____

4. What people or things are currently competing with God for attention and affection in your life?

_____

_____

_____

For I am jealous for you with a godly jealousy; for I betrothed you to one husband, so that to Christ I might present you as a pure virgin. But I am afraid that, as the serpent deceived Eve by his craftiness, your minds will be led astray from the simplicity and purity of devotion to Christ.

2 Corinthians 11:2–3

"As women who want to follow Jesus and learn to be more like Him every day, we have to make a conscious decision to grow in relationship to God and to know Him like no other" (p. 61).

5. Paul emphasizes the exclusive nature of our love relationship with Christ in 2 Corinthians 11:2–3. What does it mean to have a love relationship with Christ that is simple, pure, and devoted? Write your thoughts below.

_____

_____

6. God wants us to allow Him to fill our need for love instead of looking to others first. Meditate on Romans 5:5. How has God filled your heart to overflowing with love?

_____

_____

_____

"He longs to have fellowship with us, His precious royal daughters. He longs to see that the very first place we look to for help and reassurance is in Him" (p. 64).

7. Contemplate Luke 10:27. Consider how our love relationship with God could engage every part of who we are—body, mind, and spirit. How can you show God your love using all three areas?

_____

_____

_____

"God is in the process of making you what He wants you to be—body, mind, and spirit. He has created you to be a woman of excellence" (pp. 64–65).

8. Take some time to reflect on what God's Word says about our love relationship with Him. Review Scriptures we've studied as well as any others you wish to include here. See Hosea 2:19; John 3:16; Romans 5:8; 8:38–39 for further study.

_____

_____

_____

APPLYING GOD'S TRUTH

9. How are you tempted to compromise the "simplicity and purity of devotion" to Christ alone? What other things have captured your primary affection? Confess these in a prayer to God below.

_____

_____

_____

RECORDING KEY INSIGHTS

10. What verses or insights from today's study were particularly significant to you? Write them below and journal about what they mean to you.

_____

_____

_____

TAKING ACTION

11. What will you do differently as a result of today's study?

_____

_____

_____

SETTING THE STONE

Allow these verses to inspire your prayerful response to God today:

☐ **Psalm 4:2**—That I will not compromise my love for God today or give Him less than first place in my heart.

☐ **John 14:21**—That I will show God how much I love Him by obeying what He wants me to do.

☐ **1 John 4:10–11**—That I will remember the first One who ever loved me will always love me.

Journal notes

Journal notes

PART II

LIES WE BELIEVE

Refer to chapter 4 in *A Jewel in His Crown*.

*G*EM OF THE DAY

"You see, there are certain women that Satan knows he can fool.
There are some women who are so worldly minded that he knows he already
has them under control. But he feels challenged by those of us who dare to
think that we are truly God's daughters" (p. 72).

1. When it comes to spiritual deception, do you think Satan considers you a challenge or easy prey? Why?

_____

_____

*U*NDERSTANDING GOD'S WORD

2. Read through the story of the Fall in Genesis 3, slowly and deliberately. Reflect on the strategy Satan used to deceive Eve. Why did he go to her first? What was his intent?

_____

_____

He was a murderer from the beginning, and does not stand in the truth because there is no truth in him. Whenever he speaks a lie, he speaks from his own nature, for he is a liar and the father of lies.
John 8:44

3. Focus on the first five verses of Genesis 3. Satan's first trick was to cast doubt on God's character. Then he progressed to telling outright lies about what God said. Jesus exposed this strategy of Satan's in John 8:44. What are some of the lies Satan has been trying to get you to believe about God's character, His plans for you, or His abilities?

_____

_____

_____

"Genesis 3:13 says that the devil 'deceived' her. That same serpent wants to deceive you too" (p. 72).

4. Satan doesn't limit his libelous efforts to God alone. He also lies about God's children. According to Revelation 12:9, his goal is to deceive the whole world. What does Satan hope to accomplish with this strategy?

_____

_____

_____

**_And the great dragon was thrown down, the serpent of old who is called the devil and Satan, who deceives the whole world.
Revelation 12:9_**

5. Women in the King's court have to be on their guard against deception. Study the following verses and reflect on why Scripture adamantly instructs us to beware of falsehood.

Galatians 6:7 _____

Ephesians 5:6 _____

2 Thessalonians 2:3 _____

1 John 3:7 _____

"Unfortunately, anything that God wants to do that is pure and holy and beautiful, Satan wants to destroy" (p. 71).

6. How did Satan's deception steal, kill, and destroy the life Eve had in the Garden (see Genesis 3:16–24)?

_____

_____

_____

"Adam and Eve were His obedient children whom He loved. He gave them everything they wanted and needed. Surely they didn't really need access to that one tree, did they?" (p. 70).

*A*PPLYING GOD'S TRUTH

7. Satan can never take away our royal standing once we are in the King's court. But what has he tried to "steal, kill, and destroy" in your life and in your spiritual development as a daughter of the King?

_____

_____

_____

8. Based on what you have studied so far, identify some of the lies Satan has used to try to deceive you. After you have listed them below, journal about how you can counteract these lies with truth from God's Word.

_____

_____

_____

*The thief comes only to steal and kill and destroy; I came that they may have life, and have it abundantly.
John 10:10*

*R*ECORDING KEY INSIGHTS

9.   What verses or insights from today's study were particularly significant to you? Write them below and journal about what they mean to you.

_____

_____

_____

*T*AKING ACTION

10. What will you do differently as a result of today's study?

_____

_____

_____

SETTING THE STONE

Allow these verses to inspire your prayerful response to God today:

☐ *John 14:6*—That I will turn to Jesus and His Word to know what to believe about myself and about God.

☐ *Titus 3:3*—That I will not give in to Satan's foolish lies.

☐ *2 John 1:7*—That I will be on my guard against others whom Satan might use to deceive me.

Journal notes

Journal notes

CHOOSE TO
BE CONTENT

Refer to chapter 4 in *A Jewel in His Crown*.

*G*EM OF THE DAY

"One very old trick is this: The devil seeks to get you to do, be, or have
anything that God has not called you to do, be, or have" (p. 71).

1.   Describe how a woman who is "content" in every area of her life acts and thinks.
     Consider areas such as her relationships, her personal values, her checkbook, her
     manner of dress, her conversation with others, use of her time, etc.

Not that I speak
from want, for I
have learned to be
content in whatever
circumstances I am.
Philippians 4:11

_____

_____

_____

*U*NDERSTANDING GOD'S WORD

2.   When Paul wrote to the Philippian church, he had been unjustly imprisoned. And
     yet he could say he was content. What does this teach us about the relationship
     between outward circumstances and inner contentment? Write your thoughts below.

_____

_____

_____

3. The Bible warns us about discontentment. What do you learn by studying the following Scriptures?

Luke 21:34 _____

Philippians 2:14 _____

1 Timothy 6:6–10 _____

"Sometimes we look at the woman who got what we wanted and we say, 'What does she have that I don't have?' This is where jealousy is born" (p. 71).

4. Discontentment exposes us to all kinds of temptations: marital infidelity, greed, envy, depression. Don't let the devil use discontentment to disparage God's blessings. Meditate on the following verses that remind you how to find your soul's satisfaction in God alone. Write your thoughts below.

Psalm 34:10 _____

Psalm 107:9 _____

Jeremiah 31:14 _____

Joel 2:26 _____

But godliness actually is a means of great gain when accompanied by contentment.
1 Timothy 6:6

"You need to understand that the closer you are to the Lord, the harder the devil will attempt to trick you and snare you in his traps" (p. 72).

5. Take some time to reflect on what God's Word says about contentment. Review Scriptures we've studied as well as any others you wish to include here.

_____

_____

_____

"God will steer us away from the plots and plans of that colorful, slithering creature who—after all these years—is still making promises he can't keep" (p. 77).

$\mathcal{A}$PPLYING GOD'S TRUTH

6. In what areas of your life are you most vulnerable to feeling discontent? What advice from Scripture will help you guard against those feelings?

_____

_____

_____

7. Strengthen your resolve against discontent by writing a letter to God thanking Him for all that He has given you. You may want to refer to Hebrews 13:5 for inspiration.

_____

_____

_____

$\mathcal{R}$ECORDING KEY INSIGHTS

8. What verses or insights from today's study were particularly significant to you? Write them below and journal about what they mean to you.

_____

_____

_____

$\mathcal{T}$AKING ACTION

9. What will you do differently as a result of today's study?

_____

_____

_____

SETTING THE STONE

Allow these verses to inspire your prayerful response to God today:

☐ *Genesis 25:8*—That I will be satisfied with the life God has given me.

☐ *Psalm 37:3–5*—That God will replace my desires with His.

☐ *Jeremiah 31:14*—That I will be satisfied with God's goodness.

☐ *2 Corinthians 12:10*—That I will not allow circumstances to determine my happiness.

Journal notes

Journal notes

PART 13

DISTRACTIONS, DISTRACTIONS!

Refer to chapter 4 in A Jewel in His Crown.

*G*EM OF THE DAY

"[Satan] often tries to get us so bothered by the one thing we have been
commanded by God not to do, that we spend far too much time thinking about it.
Ultimately it distracts us from obeying God in other areas" (p. 73).

1. Are you easily distracted when you have a goal in mind? Why or why not?

_____

_____

_____

*U*NDERSTANDING GOD'S WORD

2. Read Genesis 2:16–17. What did the Lord give Adam and Eve freedom to do? How
   does this compare with what He commanded them not to do?

_____

_____

_____

3. Eve was so overcome by curiosity and attraction to the one forbidden tree in the Garden of Eden that she was distracted from all her other blessings. What "forbidden trees" have you been attracted to? How are they keeping you from enjoying all the other things that God has given you the freedom to explore?

_____

_____

_____

"She had the enjoyment of all of the other trees in the Garden, but she just couldn't get her mind off of that one thing that she wasn't supposed to have" (p. 75).

4. We sometimes feel like God's commands cramp our style! But God's Word says that His commands are for our good. Read and reflect on the Scriptures below.

Psalm 19:8 _____

Psalm 119:127–128 _____

Proverbs 7:1–2 _____

Isaiah 1:19 _____

John 15:10 _____

"We become so preoccupied with certain restrictions that God has placed on our lives that we forget, just as Eve did, that those restrictions are for our own good" (p. 73).

5. If the devil can't deceive us or make us discontent, he will try distracting us to get our minds off of what God wants us to do. Read Hebrews 12:1–2. What is God asking you to do that you need to fix your eyes on?

_____

_____

_____

"What joy there is in simply enjoying what God has for us right now. But in order to do that, we must not be consumed with what He has asked us not to do" (p. 73).

Brethren, I do not regard myself as having laid hold of it yet; but one thing I do: forgetting what lies behind and reaching forward to what lies ahead, I press on toward the goal for the prize of the upward call of God in Christ Jesus. Philippians 3:13–14

6. Meditate on Paul's inspiring words in Philippians 3:12–14. What would it mean to press on toward all God has in mind for you to do? Journal your thoughts below.

_____

_____

_____

7. Take some time to reflect on what God's Word says about abandoning distractions and focusing on Him. Review Scriptures we've studied as well as any others you wish to include here.

_____

_____

_____

$\mathcal{A}$PPLYING GOD'S TRUTH

8. How do you generally respond to the boundaries God places on your life? Do you thrive within the boundaries he has provided for your sexuality, finances, relationships, etc., or are you burdened by them? Journal your thoughts below.

_____

_____

_____

9. What have been the biggest distractions from God's ultimate purposes and plans for you? Write a prayer confessing what God reveals to you. Commit to seeking His will for your life.

_____

_____

_____

Recording Key Insights

10. What verses or insights from today's study were particularly significant to you? Write them below and journal about what they mean to you.

_____

_____

_____

Taking Action

11. What will you do differently as a result of today's study?

_____

_____

_____

SETTING THE STONE

Allow these verses to inspire your prayerful response to God today:

☐ **Psalm 141:8**—That I will keep my eyes on God and what He has for me instead of life's distractions.

☐ **2 Corinthians 4:18**—For the ability to see things in my life from God's perspective, not just my earthly vantage point.

☐ **1 John 5:3**—That I will recognize God's commands are not burdensome, but they are for my good.

Journal notes

Journal notes

PART 14

JEWELS
IN THE MUD

Refer to chapter 5 in *A Jewel in His Crown*.

*G*EM OF THE DAY

"By God's grace, we don't need to cling to the guilt and shame that keep us from reaching our full potential. Maybe you cannot forget, but you can recover and move on" (p. 80).

1. What have you done that you still haven't forgiven yourself for?

   _____

   _____

2. Why do you think we have such a difficult time forgiving ourselves—even after God has forgiven us?

   _____

   _____

*U*NDERSTANDING GOD'S WORD

3. Remembering what Jesus did in order to secure God's forgiveness can help us when we struggle to believe that we've really been forgiven. Carefully read through Hebrews 10:10–18. Be sure to note all that Jesus accomplished for us through His sacrifice on the cross. Record what you find.

> *Therefore, brethren, since we have confidence to enter the holy place by the blood of Jesus, . . . let us draw near with a sincere heart in full assurance of faith, having our hearts sprinkled clean from an evil conscience and our bodies washed with pure water.*
> *Hebrews 10:19, 22*

_____

_____

_____

4. Now, continue reading in Hebrews 10:19–22. How does the Bible describe the way in which daughters of the King ought to approach His throne? Why are they able to do so?

_____

_____

_____

"The reason most people remain in the tragedies of the past is that they do not think they are worth the effort that it takes to move on" (p. 81).

5. Read about your worth and the great price God paid for you in Matthew 10:31, 1 Corinthians 6:19–20, and Revelation 5:9, and journal your response below.

For he who lacks these qualities is blind or short-sighted, having forgotten his purification from his former sins.
2 Peter 1:9

_____

_____

_____

"If you fell into a mud puddle, you wouldn't stay there, would you? You would want to get out as soon as possible and clean yourself up. You would want to go home and take a shower and put on different clothes" (p. 81).

6. Read the following Scriptures and meditate on how Christ cleanses us from sin and makes us a bright and sparkling jewel in His crown. Journal your response to each verse.

Isaiah 1:18 _____

Ephesians 5:25–26 _____

2 Peter 1:5–9 _____

7. Read Matthew 8:1–3 about a man cleansed from a terrible disease that covered his body. Put the man's plea in verse 2 into your own words as a prayer to the Lord.

_____

_____

_____

8. Just as He cleansed the man of a terrible disease, Jesus is also willing and able to cleanse *you,* no matter how terrible your past sin may be. Take some time to reflect on what God's Word says about receiving His forgiveness and moving forward in life. Review Scriptures we've studied as well as any others you wish to include here.

_____

_____

_____

$\mathcal{A}$PPLYING GOD'S TRUTH

"Maybe there were circumstances beyond your immediate control that challenged your proper sense of self. . . . But, my friend, it is your fault if you have not recovered from that by allowing the Lord to heal you. I know that that may sound harsh. But Scripture reveals that we have the power in Christ Jesus to rid ourselves of the effects of the past" (pp. 79–80).

If we confess our sins, He is faithful and righteous to forgive us our sins and to cleanse us from all unrighteousness.
1 John 1:9

9. In what way(s) do you feel "stuck in the mud" of guilt and sin?

_____

_____

_____

10. Based on what you have learned so far, what is your response to the cleansing power of Jesus?

_____

_____

_____

RECORDING KEY INSIGHTS

11. What verses or insights from today's study were particularly significant to you? Write them below and journal about what they mean to you.

_____

_____

_____

TAKING ACTION

12. What will you do differently as a result of today's study?

_____

_____

_____

SETTING THE STONE

Allow these verses to inspire your prayerful response to God today:

☐ *Psalm 19:12–14*—That God, not my sins, will rule over me.

☐ *Psalm 25:7; Hebrews 8:12*—That I can forget my past sins just as God has.

☐ *Colossians 1:13–15*—That I will praise Jesus, who has forgiven my sins.

☐ *Hebrews 9:14*—That I will allow Jesus to cleanse my guilty conscience.

Journal notes

Journal notes

PART 15

GET MOVING

Refer to chapter 5 in *A Jewel in His Crown*.

𝒢EM OF THE DAY

*"I don't want to attend any pity party, especially one that is about me. Why?
Because as God's chosen women, we should want others to see us moving
about our lives with a noble bearing" (p. 82).*

1. Describe the last pity party you were a part of—either your own or someone else's.

_____

_____

_____

𝒰NDERSTANDING GOD'S WORD

2. Read the story of the woman caught in adultery in John 8:3–11. Contrast Jesus'
reaction with the crowd's response. Pay special attention to Jesus' parting words to
her in verse 11.

_____

_____

*For those who are
according to the
flesh set their
minds on the
things of the flesh,
but those who are
according to the
Spirit, the things
of the Spirit.
Romans 8:5*

3. Sure, even women in the King's court mess up royally! But once they realize their
sin, they confess it, repent of it and move forward. Read and reflect on Romans
8:1–15. What are the differences between a life controlled by the Spirit and one controlled by the sinful nature?

_____

_____

_____

"In special seasons of prayer, I have requested that the Lord remove my filthy garments from me and dress me in spotless, new clothes that will remind both myself and others of my worth and value" (p. 82).

4. Read about our "new clothes" in the following verses. Imagine yourself donning the garments described in Scripture and reflect on how good you look and, more important, how good you feel in those new clothes!

    Romans 13:14 _____

    Galatians 3:27 _____

    Colossians 3:12 _____

"The God of the universe wants to clothe you in robes of righteousness" (p. 82).

5. If you've struggled with being spiritually stagnant, meditate on God's promise to move you forward in faith in Isaiah 58:8–11. What does God say He will do for you?

    _____

    _____

    _____

And the LORD will continually guide you, And satisfy your desire in scorched places, And give strength to your bones; And you will be like a watered garden, And like a spring of water whose waters do not fail.
Isaiah 58:11

6. Take some time to reflect on what God's Word says about being forgiven and moving forward in faith. Review Scriptures we've studied as well as any others you wish to include here.

    _____

    _____

    _____

*A*PPLYING GOD'S TRUTH

7. If we're going to stay out of the mud puddles, we have to learn to walk down different paths. Are there certain patterns to your love relationships, finances, friendships, etc., that go against God's Word and land you in the same old mud puddles every time? If you can, describe these patterns below.

_____

_____

_____

8. Read James 1:5. Ask the Holy Spirit for wisdom to avoid old sin patterns and find a bright new path in which to walk. What are the first steps you need to take? Describe how and when you will begin.

_____

_____

_____

RECORDING KEY INSIGHTS

9. What verses or insights from today's study were particularly significant to you? Write them below and journal about what they mean to you.

_____

_____

_____

TAKING ACTION

10. What will you do differently as a result of today's study?

_____

_____

_____

SETTING THE STONE

Allow these verses to inspire your prayerful response to God today:

☐ *John 5:14*—That God will help me let go of the habitual sins I'm hanging on to.

☐ *John 8:10–11*—That I can move forward in life free from the guilt of past sins.

☐ *Ephesians 5:9–11*—That I will put my energy toward pleasing God.

☐ *Hebrews 11:24–26*—That I will choose to please God instead of pursuing the short-term pleasure of sin.

Journal notes

Journal notes

PART 16

FIGHTING TO WIN

Refer to chapter 5 in *A Jewel in His Crown*.

Gem of the Day

*"As long as we are on this earth we will be attached to our fleshly bodies.
And the only way to outsmart the flesh is to have a spirit that is stronger" (p. 91).*

1. Imagine that you are giving a report from the front lines of the ongoing battle inside of you between the flesh (what you naturally want to do) and the Spirit (what God wants you to do). Which side is currently winning? Are your spiritual troops retreating or advancing?

_____

_____

> *For the flesh sets its desire against the Spirit, and the Spirit against the flesh; for these are in opposition to one another, so that you may not do the things that you please.*
> *Galatians 5:17*

Understanding God's Word

2. Read Galatians 5:17. Reflect on the dilemma Scripture describes. Why is it so difficult to accomplish what God wants us to do?

_____

_____

3. Paul gives us insight into the universal human struggle with sin in Romans 7:14–18 by referring to his own experience. How would you put his confession into your own words?

4. One thing we can do to turn the tide in this battle is to stop arming the fleshly side of our nature. Study Galatians 5:19–21. List some of the weaponry the flesh uses to wage war against our spirits. How have you seen evidence of this in your life recently?

5. Now take a look at Galatians 5:22–25. The second goal is to build up the artillery of the Spirit. How could the things mentioned here successfully combat and overcome the flesh?

For I know that nothing good dwells in me, that is, in my flesh; for the willing is present in me, but the doing of the good is not.
Romans 7:18

"We simply feed our flesh and ignore our spirit. We must reverse the situation by nourishing our spirit through prayer, fasting, and continuous Bible reading, while starving our flesh so that it can be overcome" (p. 92).

6. Read Romans 8:1–2. What has Jesus promised the battle-weary soldier? What encouragement can you find for your spiritual battle in this passage?

"It is impossible not to struggle with the flesh while we are here on earth. *We will always have to remain cognizant of our walk in the Spirit*" (p. 93).

7. Take some time to reflect on what God's Word says about the battle between the flesh and the spirit. Review Scriptures we've studied as well as any others you wish to include here.

_____

_____

$\mathcal{A}$PPLYING GOD'S TRUTH

8. In what specific situations in your life is the battle between flesh and spirit currently raging? How does today's study of God's Word affect your strategy for handling these conflicts?

_____

_____

9. Our flesh gains power when we feed it with negative influences—certain kinds of TV shows, movies, books, music, and other entertainment. Although there is nothing wrong with having fun, we must be careful to guard what we allow ourselves to see and hear. In what ways have you been feeding the flesh? How can you feed your spirit instead?

_____

_____

Now those who belong to Christ Jesus have crucified the flesh with its passions and desires. If we live by the Spirit, let us also walk by the Spirit.
Galatians 5:24–25

RECORDING KEY INSIGHTS

10. What verses or insights from today's study were particularly significant to you? Write them below and journal about what they mean to you.

_____

_____

_____

TAKING ACTION

11. What will you do differently as a result of today's study?

....

....

....

SETTING THE STONE

Allow these verses to inspire your prayerful response to God today:

☐ *Mark 8:34–36*—That I will see my eternal reward is far greater than any temporary gain from fleshly desires.

☐ *Ephesians 4:22–24*—For God to renew me from the inside out.

☐ *Ephesians 6:13*—That I will prepare myself spiritually and put on the full armor of God before facing my battles.

☐ *Colossians 3:5–10*—That I will put my earthly desires to death and strive to please God instead of myself.

Journal notes

Journal notes

PART 17

HEALING FROM HEARTBREAK

Refer to chapter 6 in *A Jewel in His Crown*.

Gem of the Day

*"We long to be in a relationship in which we are needed, loved, and cherished.
But ironically, the very thing we were created to do, the very thing we want to do most,
is the very thing that often contributes to our low self-esteem" (p. 98).*

1. Think back on a time of personal heartbreak. What did you learn from the experience?

    _____

    _____

    _____

"For I know the plans that I have for you," declares the LORD, "plans for welfare and not for calamity to give you a future and a hope." Jeremiah 29:11

Understanding God's Word

2. At one time or another, most of us have endured a broken heart as a result of a relationship. Read the following Scriptures and journal your thoughts about God being close to those who are brokenhearted.

    Psalm 34:18 _____

    Psalm 147:3 _____

    Isaiah 61:1 _____

3.   Usually we can only blame ourselves for times we have gone against God's instructions (and, in hindsight, our better judgment) to pursue a relationship that was less than God's best. If we don't feel like we are worth God's best, we may be willing to "take what we can get." Take some time to meditate on Jeremiah 29:11. In your relationships, do you typically follow your own road map, or do you trust God's plans for you?

_____

_____

_____

"Are you settling for less than the best? You are a jewel in Jesus' crown, and you deserve to be treated with dignity" (p. 106).

4.   Our self-esteem problems often lead to relationship problems. Do you see the connection? Read Isaiah 55:2. When we invest time and energy into the wrong human relationships (expecting them to make us finally feel good about ourselves), we end up dissatisfied. When have you experienced this or seen it happen to others?

Why do you spend money for what is not bread, And your wages for what does not satisfy? Listen carefully to Me, and eat what is good, And delight yourself in abundance.

Isaiah 55:2

_____

_____

_____

5.   When your soul is satisfied with Jesus' love, your heart will begin to heal and your self-esteem will grow. Then you will be ready and able to receive a human love relationship God has for you—in His time. Meditate on John 15:9–10 and journal about what it means to abide, or "stay," inside of Jesus' love for you.

_____

_____

_____

"Sister, do you understand that you and I deserve the best simply because Christ says we do?" (p. 106).

6. Take some time to reflect on what God's Word says about low self-esteem and poor decisions—especially in our love relationships. Review Scriptures we've studied as well as any others you wish to include here.

$\mathcal{A}$PPLYING GOD'S TRUTH

7. What relationships have you been using to try to fill your need for love? In view of the way God loves you and the wonderful plans He has for your life, how should this pattern change?

8. Take some time now to write a prayer of confession to the Lord. Take your wounded self-esteem to Him and make a commitment to "abide" in Him and in His love as He heals your heart.

$\mathcal{R}$ECORDING KEY INSIGHTS

9. What verses or insights from today's study were particularly significant to you? Write them below and journal about what they mean to you.

*T*AKING ACTION

10. What will you do differently as a result of today's study?

_____

_____

_____

SETTING THE STONE

Allow these verses to inspire your prayerful response to God today:

☐ *Psalm 62:8*—That I will pour out my heart to the Lord.

☐ *Isaiah 55:8–9*—That I will trust and accept that His ways are better than mine.

☐ *Zephaniah 3:17*—For me to realize that God delights in me!

Journal notes

Journal notes

PART 18

LEARNING TO WAIT

Refer to chapter 6 in *A Jewel in His Crown*.

GEM OF THE DAY

*"We talk the talk! We look spiritual . . . but when push comes to shove, our lack
of patience simply means that all our great talking we do is just that . . . talk.
We don't really trust that He is able" (p. 106).*

1. Finish this statement regarding your level of patience:
   When it comes to having patience, those who know me best would say I definitely . . .

   _____

   _____

   _____

*I wait for the LORD,
my soul does wait,
And in His word do
I hope.
Psalm 130:5*

UNDERSTANDING GOD'S WORD

2. Waiting on God's timing is something every believer struggles with at one time or
   another. Read how the psalmist felt about waiting on God. Can you relate? Write
   about your own similar feelings and experiences beside each Scripture.

   Psalm 25:5 _____

   Psalm 27:13–14 _____

   Psalm 39:7 _____

   Psalm 40:1 _____

   Psalm 130:5 _____

"You need to trust Him through patient obedience as you wait on Him" (p. 107).

3. God has incredible blessings in store for each woman in his court. But patience is essential. Read Hebrews 6:11–12. Ask the Lord to give you the power to have faith until you inherit His great promises.

_____

_____

_____

"If we are afraid to wait on God to give us the best, then we don't really believe that He'll do what He says He will do" (p. 106).

4. Is God able to do what He says He will do? That's the question, isn't it? We're not the first ones to wonder. Spend some time meditating on what God said to Job in Job 38. Write out the phrases in the passage that demonstrate His boundless power.

_____

_____

_____

Where were you when I laid the foundation of the earth? Tell Me, if you have understanding, Who set its measurements? Since you know. Or who stretched the line on it?

Job 38:4–5

5. I challenge you to wait for God's best. You will be so glad you did! Review Scriptures we've studied as well as any others you wish to include here. You may refer to Colossians 1:11; 3:12; James 5:7 for further study.

_____

_____

_____

*A*PPLYING GOD'S TRUTH

6. In what ways have you settled for less than God's best—especially in regard to relationships?

_____

_____

_____

7. If God were to speak to you the way He spoke to Job in Job 38, what examples could He use to remind you of the limitless power He has already exerted in your own life?

8. Based on what you've studied so far, what does it mean to wait for God's best in every area of your life? Are you willing to do this? Why or why not? Spend some time in honest prayer before the Lord, confess any impatience or independence from Him, and recommit yourself to receiving only God's best.

9. Make a list of the things that you are currently settling for in your life because you aren't trusting completely in His ability to give you the best.

RECORDING KEY INSIGHTS

10. What verses or insights from today's study were particularly significant to you? Write them below and journal about what they mean to you.

*T*AKING ACTION

11. What will you do differently as a result of today's study?

_____

_____

_____

SETTING THE STONE

Allow these verses to inspire your prayerful response to God today:

☐ *Psalm 5:8*—That I will acknowledge God as my leader.

☐ *Psalm 37:7*—That I will entrust my worries to God's care.

☐ *Isaiah 40:31*—For God to strengthen me as I wait on Him.

☐ *Hebrews 6:15*—That I will follow Abraham's example and wait on God to fulfill His promises.

Journal notes

Journal notes

AH, MEN!

Refer to chapter 6 in *A Jewel in His Crown*.

𝒢EM OF THE DAY

*"How many times will you allow your heart to be broken and re-mended before
you just decide to let God do the choosing for you?" (p. 109).*

1. Whether you are married or single, what frustrates you the most about your love life
    right now?

    _____

    _____

𝒰NDERSTANDING GOD'S WORD

*Watch over
your heart with
all diligence,
For from it
flow the
springs of life.
Proverbs 4:23*

2. God's Word is inspiring, reassuring, and very practical. Let's look at some basic bib-
    lical principles of relating to the opposite sex. To start, we must recognize this as an
    area no Christian woman enters casually. In fact, we must always be on our guard.
    Read Proverbs 4:23. What does it mean to "watch over" your heart?

    _____

    _____

    _____

3. In what ways have you not been watching over it closely enough?

    _____

    _____

    _____

4. Our culture values the aggressive, self-made woman, who sees something she wants and goes after it. The Christian woman doesn't fit that description. Make a list below, contrasting the guidelines found in 1 Peter 3:4 with what society says an ideal woman is like. Are you more like the woman described in Scripture or society's ideal woman?

_____

_____

_____

"We are never, and I mean never, *to throw ourselves at a man. It doesn't matter what our intentions may be, whether we hope to develop a romantic relationship with him or only a friendship"* (p. 110).

5. When it comes to working for the things we want in life and love, the Bible prescribes a unique division of labor. God's job? As we have learned, He is at work all the time. Our job? Psalm 46:10 explains it well. Journal your thoughts regarding this principle below.

_____

_____

_____

Then [Naomi] said, "Wait, my daughter, until you know how the matter turns out; for the man will not rest until he has settled it today."

Ruth 3:18

"A woman's job is to be still and trust the Lord. This doesn't mean sitting still and doing nothing. It means keeping yourself occupied, doing what the Lord has called you to do right now" (p. 112).

6. Let's look at an example of a woman who handled a love relationship well. You'll enjoy studying the short story of Ruth in the book that bears her name as its title. As you read, notice Ruth's patience, her willingness to leave the "pursuing" to her love interest, Boaz (see Ruth 3:18), and her diligence in her job while she was waiting. What do you learn from her example?

_____

_____

_____

7. What has God given you to occupy your time right now? Are you busy doing it?

_____

_____

_____

8. Take some time to reflect on what God's Word says about relationships between men and women. Review Scriptures we've studied as well as any others you wish to include here. Refer to Ephesians 5:22–28; 1 Timothy 3:11; 1 Peter 3:1 for further study.

_____

_____

_____

$\mathcal{A}$PPLYING GOD'S TRUTH

9. How does your typical *"modus operandi"* compare with what Scripture teaches about relationships with the opposite sex?

_____

_____

_____

10. Write a prayer of commitment to the biblical division of labor when it comes to experiencing the love of your life: While God works, you wait.

_____

_____

_____

PART 19

Ah, Men!

Recording Key Insights

11. What verses or insights from today's study were particularly significant to you? Write them below and journal about what they mean to you.

_____

_____

_____

Taking Action

12. What will you do differently as a result of today's study?

....

....

....

SETTING THE STONE

Allow these verses to inspire your prayerful response to God today:

☐ *Zechariah 4:6*—That I will rely on the Holy Spirit's power instead of my own.

☐ *John 9:4*—That I will focus on doing God's work.

☐ *1 Corinthians 6:18*—That I will stay sexually pure in thought and deed.

☐ *Ephesians 4:18–20*—That my heart will soften toward God's leadership in this area of my life.

Journal notes

Journal notes

THE ROYAL TREATMENT

Refer to chapter 7 in *A Jewel in His Crown*.

*G*EM OF THE DAY

"A princess in the King's court can expect to receive the royal treatment from her heavenly Father" (p. 117).

1. How has your relationship with your earthly father positively or negatively influenced your concept of your heavenly Father?

_____

_____

_____

"Truly, truly, I say to you, if you ask the Father for anything in My name, He will give it to you."
John 16:23

*U*NDERSTANDING GOD'S WORD

2. When Jesus talked about God, He described Him as a loving and perfect Father. Using the following Scriptures, meditate on Jesus' relationship with His heavenly Father, and journal what you learn about that relationship.

Matthew 11:27 _____

John 3:35 _____

John 16:23 _____

3. Sadly, many people's experiences with their earthly fathers have confused their understandings of their heavenly Father. Describe your relationship with your earthly father and how that has shaped your view of your heavenly Father. What about your earthly father do you need to separate from your view of God the Father?

_____

_____

_____

4. As much as we need to see God as our Father, it's equally important that we perceive ourselves as His children. We are His heirs—adopted into His kingdom. Do you realize what that means? Study the following Scriptures and rejoice over all you are entitled to as a child of the King!

Romans 8:17 _____

Galatians 3:29 _____

Ephesians 3:6 _____

Every good thing given and every perfect gift is from above, coming down from the Father of lights, with whom there is no variation or shifting shadow.
James 1:17

"As a daughter of the King, as a joint heir with Christ, she can be sure that nothing is too good for her. When she receives something from the Lord, it will be better than anything she would think to ask for, because He knows her so well and has resources she can't even imagine" (p. 117).

5. The Bible is clear about our heavenly Father's willingness to shower us with blessings. Why does he want to bless us? Because He loves us so much. That's it. No strings attached. Read James 1:17 and Matthew 7:11. Spend some time thanking and praising your Father for these promises from His Word. What are some of the "good things" the Lord has already given to you?

_____

_____

_____

Applying God's Truth

6. A princess in God's kingdom relates to the King as her Father. What privileges have you been granted in His Word that you've been ignoring or forgetting? How can you begin living out your royal status?

_____

_____

_____

7. Using some of the truths and images from your study, write a love letter to God. Thank Him for loving you and being such a wonderful Father to His children.

_____

_____

_____

Recording Key Insights

8. What verses or insights from today's study were particularly significant to you? Write them below and journal about what they mean to you.

_____

_____

_____

Taking Action

9. What will you do differently as a result of today's study?

_____

_____

_____

SETTING THE STONE

Allow these verses to inspire your prayerful response to God today:

☐ ***Deuteronomy 26:18***—That God will help me realize that I am a treasure to Him.

☐ ***Isaiah 43:4***—That I will understand I am so precious in God's sight that Jesus gave His life for my sake.

☐ ***Matthew 11:27***—For Jesus to help me understand the concept of God as my heavenly Father.

☐ ***Hebrews 6:17***—That I will remember I am an heir to all of God's promises.

Journal notes

Journal notes

PART 21

NICKELS AND DIMES

Refer to chapter 7 in *A Jewel in His Crown*.

*G*EM OF THE DAY

*"How many times have you cried and fought for a nickel
when God wanted to give you a dime?"* (p. 119).

1. What God wants to give us is always far more valuable than what we are asking Him for. Think of an example of a time when God surprised you with His will, and it turned out to be better than what you had wanted.

_____

_____

*U*NDERSTANDING GOD'S WORD

2. Sometimes we are clinging so tightly to our own good ideas and plans that we ignore God's offer to give us something better. We act like a young child refusing to let go of a nickel when offered a dime. When we are too immature to understand God's ways, we must trust He has our best interests in mind (see Proverbs 3:5–6). How would you describe your level of trust in the Lord in each of the following areas? Be honest with yourself.

	Strong	Fair	Wavering
Finances	Strong	Fair	Wavering
Relationships	Strong	Fair	Wavering
Family	Strong	Fair	Wavering
Career	Strong	Fair	Wavering
Health	Strong	Fair	Wavering

"Right now, you can probably think of some guy that has been on your trail for quite some time and you haven't given him a second glance. . . . You are passing up the dime because you are more attracted to nickels. . . . I am referring to that godly man whom you are skipping over because he is too short or too tall or not fine enough or rich enough for you" (pp. 122–23).

3. God's will is often tied to the unexpected. For example, the employment opportunity we are given may not be what we thought we wanted. Or the man we're supposed to marry may not look anything like our "type." Only God knows the behind-the-scenes information, so He wants us to trust Him instead of our instincts. How is this idea evident in 1 Samuel 16:7?

_____

_____

_____

But the LORD said to Samuel, "Do not look at his appearance or at the height of his stature, because I have rejected him; for God sees not as man sees, for man looks at the outward appearance, but the LORD looks at the heart."
1 Samuel 16:7

4. The people of the world grossly underestimated Christ's value when they put Him to death at Calvary. The Bible says they rejected and despised Him—read it for yourself in Isaiah 53:3. What aspects of the person of Jesus were they completely ignoring? What were they paying attention to?

_____

_____

_____

"This is precisely the way that Christ woos us. He loves us when we aren't remotely interested in Him. He loves us anyway and pursues us continually until we finally love Him back" (p. 122).

5. God loves to amaze us. He longs to do the unexpected in our lives. Even the Messiah's arrival on earth happened in an unexpected way. Read Luke 2:12, a reference to the birth of Christ. How was Jesus' arrival packaged differently than people might have expected?

_____

_____

_____

6. What does Isaiah 55:8–9 teach you about God's mysterious, superior ways?

_____

_____

$\mathcal{A}$PPLYING GOD'S TRUTH

7. In light of this study, what situations, relationships, and opportunities may deserve a second look and some serious prayer to determine what God is trying to tell you to do?

_____

_____

_____

8. What are you holding on to right now instead of opening your clenched fist to receive the more valuable plans God has for your life? What causes you to do this? How can you let go?

_____

_____

_____

*R*ECORDING KEY INSIGHTS

9. What verses or insights from today's study were particularly significant to you? Write them below and journal about what they mean to you.

_____

_____

_____

*T*AKING ACTION

10. What will you do differently as a result of today's study?

_____

_____

_____

SETTING THE STONE

Allow these verses to inspire your prayerful response to God today:

☐ *Jeremiah 29:13*—That I will seek God with all my heart.

☐ *Lamentations 3:25*—That I will wait for God to do what's best in my life.

☐ *Hebrews 11:1*—That I will trust in what I cannot see.

Journal notes

Journal notes

PART 22

A PERFECT MATCH

Refer to chapter 7 in *A Jewel in His Crown*.

*G*EM OF THE DAY

"For a moment, set aside those things that would normally help you to make a decision concerning a man, and consider what the Lord has said in His Word" (p. 119).

1. How would a believer's approach to dating differ from a non-believer's approach?

_____

_____

_____

So husbands ought also to love their own wives as their own bodies. He who loves his own wife loves himself.
Ephesians 5:28

*U*NDERSTANDING GOD'S WORD

2. What do you learn about a husband's ideal love for his wife from your study of the following Scriptures? (If you are currently in a dating relationship, keep these principles in mind so that you can gauge how well your man exemplifies these values.)

Ephesians 5:28, 33 _____

Colossians 3:19 _____

1 Peter 3:7 _____

"If you are already married, pray that the Lord will continue to develop these characteristics in your mate" (p. 119).

3. In Ephesians 5:25 Paul compares a husband's love for his wife to the way Jesus loves the church. From a careful reading of Ephesians 5:25–29, what observations can you make regarding Jesus' love for the church?

4. A man's love for a woman should be pure, as Christ's love for the church is. Read Paul's instruction to Timothy in 1 Timothy 4:12. How should a godly man respect and contribute to a woman's purity?

"We've made some bad decisions, and sometimes our history almost destroys us through guilt. However, this guy in your life should see you as a pure woman of God just as the Lord Jesus Christ does" (p. 120).

. . . for no one ever hated his own flesh, but nourishes and cherishes it, just as Christ also does the church. Ephesians 5:29

5. Study Ephesians 5:23. Describe the husband's role as the spiritual leader of a marriage.

"Not only must he know God's Word, but he must also be able to understand it. Simply put, this man must be your spiritual leader. He must lead by example through his life and his attentiveness to God and His Word" (p. 124).

6. What boundaries does Scripture outline for sexuality before and within marriage? See Matthew 5:28; Romans 13:13; 1 Thessalonians 4:3–7; Hebrews 13:4. How well are you staying within these boundaries?

7. Take some time to reflect on what God's Word says about the relationship between a man and a woman. Review Scriptures we've studied as well as any others you wish to include here.

_____

_____

_____

$\mathcal{A}$PPLYING GOD'S TRUTH

8. In what areas have you settled for less than the biblical ideal of who your "perfect match" should be? If you are already married, what should you pray about regarding your relationship with your mate?

_____

_____

_____

9. Are you worried that you'll never meet a godly man like this? Are you afraid your marriage can never mirror these godly principles? Write out your concerns in an honest prayer, and remember—nothing is impossible with God.

_____

_____

_____

Marriage is to be held in honor among all, and the marriage bed is to be undefiled; for fornicators and adulterers God will judge.
Hebrews 13:4

$\mathcal{R}$ECORDING KEY INSIGHTS

10. What verses or insights from today's study were particularly significant to you? Write them below and journal about what they mean to you.

_____

_____

_____

Taking Action

11. What will you do differently as a result of today's study?

_____

_____

_____

SETTING THE STONE

Allow these verses to inspire your prayerful response to God today:

☐ *1 Corinthians 7:4*—For me to love my mate sacrificially.

☐ *2 Corinthians 6:6*—That my mental and sexual purity will be commendable in God's sight.

☐ *Ephesians 5:21*—That the way I handle my love relationships will honor Christ.

Journal notes

Journal notes

SUPREME SACRIFICE

Refer to chapter 7 in *A Jewel in His Crown*.

*G*EM OF THE DAY

"Sometimes God puts us through the fire in order to
test our love and devotion to Him" (p. 125).

1. What is your typical response when you're under pressure?

_____

_____

We are afflicted in
every way, but not
crushed; perplexed,
but not despairing;
persecuted, but not
forsaken; struck
down, but not
destroyed; always
carrying about in
the body the dying
of Jesus, so that the
life of Jesus also
may be manifested
in our body.
2 Corinthians
4:8–10

*U*NDERSTANDING GOD'S WORD

2. The difference between a diamond and a cubic zirconium is easily seen under pressure. A diamond is unbreakable. A cubic zirconium shatters. Read 2 Corinthians 4:8–10 and describe how a Christian woman will hold up under pressure.

_____

"Orthodoxy is the central belief of the historical Christian faith. Orthopraxy, on the other hand, is the lifestyle you put into practice as a result of that theological foundation. I have a lot of difficulty in that because it is hard to be a woman who lives right and serves God in our day and time" (p. 126).

3. Part of what makes a jewel in the King's crown so valuable is that it is such a rare find. These women don't just talk about knowing Christ; they live like they know Him. Consider Jesus' words in Matthew 7:14; Luke 9:24; 14:33. What sacrifices are required to walk the "narrow way"?

_____

_____

_____

"Are we willing to sacrifice those things that we love for the sake of Christ Jesus? I can think of many things that I am not sure I am willing to wholly give up and devote to God" (p. 126).

4. Abraham knew the power of pressure as well as the depth of spiritual sacrifice. Read the story of the test he faced in Genesis 22:1–10. Describe the last time God asked you to give up something for His sake. Were you obedient?

For the gate is small and the way is narrow that leads to life, and there are few who find it.
Matthew 7:14

_____

_____

_____

"[God] had to wait until that crucial moment between obedience and disobedience to determine whether or not Abraham was for real. Do you really want to be a woman in the King's court, or do you just want to look like one?" (p. 127).

5. Read Genesis 22:11–19. From Abraham's experience, what do you learn about how God rewards our willingness to sacrifice for His sake?

_____

_____

_____

6. Meditate on the following Scriptures regarding God's role as "Provider" and journal your thoughts beside each verse.

    Genesis 22:14 _____

    Psalm 111:5 _____

    Psalm 111:9 _____

    Isaiah 61:3 _____

7. Take some time to reflect on what God's Word says about the role of sacrifice. Review Scriptures we've studied as well as any others you wish to include here.

    _____

    _____

    _____

$\mathcal{A}$PPLYING GOD'S TRUTH

8. Has what you've studied brought to mind any "supreme sacrifice" God may want you to make? Is there anything in your life that you would be unwilling to let go? Prayerfully offer every area of your life as a sacrifice to God.

    _____

    _____

    _____

Abraham called the name of that place The LORD Will Provide, as it is said to this day, "In the mount of the LORD it will be provided." Genesis 22:14

9. What will be your next step down the narrow road of obedience or up the mountaintop of sacrifice?

    _____

    _____

    _____

RECORDING KEY INSIGHTS

10. What verses or insights from today's study were particularly significant to you? Write them below and journal about what they mean to you.

_____

_____

_____

TAKING ACTION

11. What will you do differently as a result of today's study?

_____

_____

_____

SETTING THE STONE

Allow these verses to inspire your prayerful response to God today:

☐ *Luke 18:22*—That I will focus on treasure in heaven.

☐ *Luke 18:29–30*—That I will remember any earthly sacrifice will be rewarded in heaven.

☐ *John 8:31*—For my obedience to Christ to show I am the real thing.

Journal notes

Journal notes

PART 24

FAITHFUL TO THE FINISH

Refer to chapter 8 in *A Jewel in His Crown*.

*G*EM OF THE DAY

"If almighty God can manage the universe, then He's got you covered" (p. 134).

1. Do you have a hard time finishing projects you start? Or are you a procrastinator who never starts at all? Or somewhere between?

   _____

   _____

   _____

For I am confident of this very thing, that He who began a good work in you will perfect it until the day of Christ Jesus.
Philippians 1:6

*U*NDERSTANDING GOD'S WORD

2. Read Philippians 1:6 and put this verse into your own words. How should the certainty of God's faithfulness affect your outlook on the future?

   _____

   _____

   _____

"Jesus has promised that He will be faithful to complete the good work He began in you the moment you became a woman in the King's court. You are His rare jewel, and He is determined to refine you into the most brilliant gemstone possible" (p. 134).

3. What do the following verses tell us about God's faithfulness?

Deuteronomy 7:9 _____

2 Samuel 22:26 _____

Psalm 25:10 _____

Psalm 36:5 _____

4. God will not give up on us. Likewise, we cannot afford to give up on ourselves. Meditate on James 1:3–4. What truth about perseverance do you encounter here? In what ways have you experienced this truth?

_____

_____

_____

Knowing that the testing of your faith produces endurance. And let endurance have its perfect result, so that you may be perfect and complete, lacking in nothing.
James 1:3–4

5. In what ways do the following verses encourage us to approach our spiritual journey?

1 Corinthians 9:26 _____

2 Corinthians 10:4 _____

Galatians 6:9 _____

1 Timothy 1:18–19 _____

6. Read Hebrews 12:2. What can you learn from Jesus, our example, when it comes to finishing the race before us?

_____

_____

_____

"He thinks that you are worth the effort, and He hasn't forgotten who you are. Have you?" (p. 134).

7. When we get tired and feel like giving in, it helps to have a reminder of who we are. We are jewels in the King's crown! Meditate on the following Scriptures and truths. How do these truths encourage your faith?

    John 1:12—Royal blood runs through my veins.

    1 Corinthians 12:27—I belong to the prestigious body of Christ.

    Ephesians 2:6—I am seated beside Jesus' throne.

    Philippians 3:20—I am one of heaven's royal citizens.

    Hebrews 4:14–16—Jesus welcomes and invites me into the throne room of grace.

8. Take some time to reflect on what God's Word says about faithfulness—both His and yours. Review Scriptures we've studied as well as any others you wish to include here. You may wish to refer to Romans 5:3–5 and James 5:11 for further study.

    _____

    _____

*A*PPLYING GOD'S TRUTH

9. When have you been tempted to lie down and give up the race? Pour out your heart to God regarding your reasons for retreating.

    _____

    _____

This command I entrust to you, Timothy, my son, in accordance with the prophecies previously made concerning you, that by them you fight the good fight.
1 Timothy 1:18

10. After you have spent some time praying through what you have written above, reaffirm your determination to keep going. Use the images from the Scripture you studied to write your steadfast commitment below.

    _____

    _____

    _____

Recording Key Insights

11. What verses or insights from today's study were particularly significant to you? Write them below and journal about what they mean to you.

_____

_____

_____

Taking Action

12. What will you do differently as a result of today's study?

_____

_____

_____

Fixing our eyes on Jesus, the author and perfecter of faith, who for the joy set before Him endured the cross, despising the shame, and has sat down at the right hand of the throne of God.
Hebrews 12:2

SETTING THE STONE

Allow these verses to inspire your prayerful response to God today:

☐ **Psalm 89:2**—That I will remember His faithfulness is firmly established.

☐ **2 Thessalonians 1:4**—For my perseverance to inspire others in their faith.

☐ **2 Timothy 4:7**—That I can confidently say I have fought the good fight, finished the course, and kept the faith.

☐ **2 Peter 1:6**—That I will add perseverance to the top of the list in my prayers.

Journal notes

Journal notes

PART 25

RESETTING THE STONE

Refer to chapter 8 in *A Jewel in His Crown*.

*G*EM OF THE DAY

"If you don't know you need help and aren't willing to get real with God, then you won't get anything from Him" (p. 135).

1. It's time for you to be honest with yourself and with God. List the areas of your life in which you need the Lord to "reset the stone."

   _____

   _____

   _____

For the Son of Man has come to seek and to save that which was lost.
Luke 19:10

*U*NDERSTANDING GOD'S WORD

2. Jesus was unlike any religious figure the Pharisees had ever seen. He actually loved and fellowshipped with sinners! Reflect on Jesus' actions and attitudes in Luke 19:1–10. What kind of effect did they have on Zacchaeus?

   _____

   _____

   _____

"Jesus paid special attention to those who needed Him most. He was interested in hanging out not with the Pharisees, but rather with those who were afflicted with disease and spiritual darkness" (p. 135).

3. "Resetting the stone" is the Lord's specialty. Read Mark 2:17. What has Jesus come to do?

_____

_____

_____

"Jesus wants you to be free to shine for him in a way that you never thought possible" (p. 135).

4. Meditate on the comforting image from the Old Testament prophecy about Jesus that is quoted in Matthew 12:20. In what ways are a battered reed and a smoldering wick similar? What does this teach you about Jesus?

_____

_____

_____

"A BATTERED REED [GOD] WILL NOT BREAK OFF, AND A SMOLDERING WICK HE WILL NOT PUT OUT."
Matthew 12:20

5. No one is excluded from becoming a jewel in the King's crown—no matter what sin has "tarnished" her past. Reflect on Romans 8:38–39. List all the things that cannot separate us from God's love.

_____

_____

_____

6. Still having a hard time believing that Jesus loves sinners? Read through His description of God in these three parables. Though they may be familiar to you, read each one slowly and deliberately. What observations can you draw from each about God's love?

Luke 15:1–7 _____

Luke 15:8–10 _____

Luke 15:11–24 _____

"Now let's take Jesus up on His offer to love us unconditionally, to love us right out of the pit that we've dug for ourselves" (p. 135).

7. Take some time to reflect on what God's Word says about Jesus' love for sinners. Review Scriptures we've studied as well as any others you wish to include here.

_____

_____

_____

𝒜PPLYING GOD'S TRUTH

8. Perhaps the best way to envision Jesus' love for sinners is captured in Luke 7:47. The more we have been forgiven, the greater our love for God will be. How has the sin in your past and His forgiveness increased your love for Jesus today?

_____

_____

_____

9. The Pharisees failed to understand or accept a God who passionately loved and would share a table with sinners. How has God's Word changed your perception or understanding of Jesus?

_____

_____

_____

For I am convinced that neither death, nor life, nor angels, nor principalities, nor things present, nor things to come, nor powers, nor height, nor depth, nor any other created thing, will be able to separate us from the love of God, which is in Christ Jesus our Lord.
Romans 8:38–39

RECORDING KEY INSIGHTS

10. What verses or insights from today's study were particularly significant to you? Write them below and journal about what they mean to you.

_____

_____

_____

TAKING ACTION

11. What will you do differently as a result of today's study?

_____

_____

_____

SETTING THE STONE

Allow these verses to inspire your prayerful response to God today:

☐ *2 Chronicles 7:14*—For God to heal me from my past sins.

☐ *Psalm 103:3–5*—That I am never beyond God's healing and forgiveness.

☐ *Romans 8:33–34*—That I will remember Jesus doesn't condemn me, and avoid condemning myself.

Journal notes

Journal notes

PART 26

BETTER
than BEFORE

Refer to chapter 8 in *A Jewel in His Crown*.

*G*EM OF THE DAY

*"Despite the mistakes, despite the sin, and despite the hurt and pain
that has caused your low self-estimation, He wants to reset
you and make you better than ever"* (p. 144).

1. How do you view the future? Do you believe the best is yet to come in your walk with Christ? Explain.

_____

_____

_____

*He restores
my soul;
He guides me
in the paths of
righteousness
For His name's
sake.
Psalm 23:3*

*U*NDERSTANDING GOD'S WORD

2. At times, our spiritual lives can be akin to abandoned buildings—dilapidated and worn out from neglect. Thankfully, God is in the remodeling business. Read Psalm 23:3 and journal your response to the idea that God can restore your soul.

_____

_____

_____

3. Meditate on the following additional images of restoration and revitalization. What will God do for His people as a mender, healer, and master builder?

Isaiah 9:10 _____

Isaiah 58:12 _____

Jeremiah 33:7 _____

Amos 9:11 _____

4. When the Jews decided to rebuild the temple that had been destroyed by their ene-mies and damaged through years of neglect, God promised He would help them. Read Haggai 2:7–9. How could this passage relate to your own spiritual "temple"?

_____

_____

_____

"Just like the Jews who had to rebuild their temple, you and I have to rebuild ours" (p. 144).

The bricks have fallen down, But we will rebuild with smooth stones; The sycamores have been cut down, But we will replace them with cedars.
Isaiah 9:10

5. Read John 2:19–21 and reflect on what Jesus (speaking of His own body) promised when He said God would resurrect life from death, the new from the old. What are the "dead" areas of your life that need to be resurrected by God?

_____

_____

_____

"God knows it won't be easy, but He wants you to focus on rebuilding you: your value, your worth, your potential, your self-esteem, your temple" (p. 144).

6. Read Haggai 2:9 again, written as an encouragement to the Jews, who were reluc-tant to finish rebuilding the temple. What did God promise them as a result of their efforts?

_____

_____

_____

"If you will lay aside all of the sin and encumbrances of your past and entrust the present and the future to Him, He will do more than guide you in rebuilding what has been destroyed. He will make sure your latter glory will far outshine your former glory. Isn't that amazing?" (p. 144).

7. What do the following images from God's Word teach you about spiritual renewal?

    Isaiah 43:19 _____

    Isaiah 64:4 _____

8. What can you learn about the revitalization of our spiritual lives from the following verses?

    Psalm 4:7 _____

    Psalm 40:3 _____

    Psalm 51:10 _____

*A*PPLYING GOD'S TRUTH

Behold, I will do something new, Now it will spring forth.
Isaiah 43:19

9. What can you identify as the "something new" that Scripture tells us God wants to do in your life? Ask the Holy Spirit for wisdom and guidance as you journal your response.

    _____

    _____

    _____

10. Compose a letter to God expressing your willingness to let Him lead you down a new path in your spiritual life that will far surpass anything you've experienced in the past.

    _____

    _____

    _____

    _____

*R*ECORDING KEY INSIGHTS

11. What verses or insights from today's study were particularly significant to you? Write them below and journal about what they mean to you.

_____

_____

_____

*T*AKING ACTION

12. What will you do differently as a result of today's study?

_____

_____

_____

SETTING THE STONE

Allow these verses to inspire your prayerful response to God today:

☐ *Isaiah 61:1*—For God to free me from my past so I can accept His future for me.

☐ *Lamentations 3:22–23*—For God's mercies and lovingkindness to greet me anew every morning.

☐ *Joel 2:25*—That God will restore the time I wasted living in sin.

Journal notes

Journal notes

PART 27

AN EMERALD
CALLED GRACE

Refer to chapter 9 in *A Jewel in His Crown*.

*G*EM OF THE DAY

*"It is precisely in your frailty and failure that God wants to meet with you,
to challenge you to know Him more intimately and to live more successfully,
to extend His grace to you" (p. 147).*

1. Why can't anyone earn or buy her way into the King's court?

_____

_____

*U*NDERSTANDING GOD'S WORD

2. Make no mistake, the women in the King's court are there by His grace, not because they're good enough, pretty enough, worthy enough, or wealthy enough. In fact, it's just the opposite. Read Romans 3:23–24. Why are we in such desperate need of His grace?

_____

_____

*For all have
sinned and fall
short of the glory
of God, being
justified as a gift
by His grace
through the
redemption
which is in
Christ Jesus.
Romans 3:23–24*

3. All the jewels in His crown were once helpless, ungodly, and regarded as God's enemies. Read Romans 5:6–10, and describe how you see evidence of this truth in your life.

    _____

    _____

    _____

"In His grace, He looks beyond our faults and sees our needs" (p. 147).

4. The deeper you get to know God, the more clearly you will see His holiness. Read Isaiah 6:5 and 64:6, and describe your own position in light of God's holiness.

    _____

    _____

    _____

For while we were still helpless, at the right time Christ died for the ungodly. For one will hardly die for a righteous man; though perhaps for the good man someone would dare even to die. But God demonstrates His own love toward us, in that while we were yet sinners, Christ died for us.
Romans 5:6–8

5. Scripture is clear—sin dealt us a tragic, fatal blow. According to Romans 6:23, what do we deserve?

    _____

    _____

    _____

"The grace of God demands our full attention. It is more magnificent than anything that we can imagine, yet we take God's grace far too lightly. Without it, you and I would be helpless" (p. 152).

6. If we could earn our way into royalty any other way, then Christ died "needlessly," according to Galatians 2:21. In what ways have you taken the grace of God for granted?

    _____

    _____

    _____

7. The emerald called grace becomes even more valuable to us when we see just how weak and helpless we are without it. Ponder the imagery Jesus uses in Matthew 9:36. How is this an accurate description of us?

_____

_____

_____

"No one has accomplished anything that God's grace has not allowed. Without God's grace, we can do nothing. Without it, we would perish" (p. 152).

8. Take some time to reflect on what God's Word says about why we desperately need an emerald called grace to adorn our lives. Review verses we've studied as well as any others you wish to include here.

_____

_____

_____

$\mathcal{A}$PPLYING GOD'S TRUTH

9. In what ways have you been needlessly trying to "prove" your worth to God—striving to impress Him enough by your goodness? Humbly confess these attitudes and actions in a prayer below.

_____

_____

_____

10. Based on what you've studied in God's Word, why is the emerald of grace so valuable to you?

_____

_____

_____

I do not nullify the grace of God, for if righteousness comes through the Law, then Christ died needlessly.
Galatians 2:21

*R*ECORDING KEY INSIGHTS

11. What verses or insights from today's study were particularly significant to you? Write them below and journal about what they mean to you.

_____

_____

_____

*T*AKING ACTION

12. What will you do differently as a result of today's study?

_____

_____

_____

SETTING THE STONE

Allow these verses to inspire your prayerful response to God today:

☐ ***Ephesians 3:8***—For me to see myself as a needy candidate for God's grace because of my weakness.

☐ ***Philippians 3:7***—That I would not forfeit God's grace by clinging to my own righteousness.

☐ ***Titus 3:4–6***—For me to count my good deeds and my striving to impress God as worthless.

☐ ***1 John 1:8***—That I will gladly recognize myself as a sinner in need of God's grace.

Journal notes

Journal notes

God Made a Way

Refer to chapter 9 in *A Jewel in His Crown*.

Gem of the Day

"God's emerald of grace sparkles and shines in our lives, making us more beautiful and valuable than we could ever be without it" (p. 147).

1. What is the best Christmas present or birthday gift you've ever received, and why? How did you treat this gift?

_____

_____

_____

Understanding God's Word

2. God made a way to transform the dime-store, costume jewelry of humanity into a priceless jewel in His crown—through His free gift of love. Write the second half of Romans 6:23 below.

_____

_____

For by grace you have been saved through faith; and that not of yourselves, it is the gift of God, not as a result of works, so that no one may boast.
Ephesians 2:8–9

"He gave up His heavenly home and came to earth not just to live among us but also to die for us" (p. 154).

3. Read the following verses about God's rich mercy and great love, and write a simple summary of the message and its meaning to you.

   Ephesians 2:4–5 _____

   Ephesians 2:8–9 _____

4. Meditate on the simple but profound truth in John 3:16–17. If you had to explain how God has provided a way for salvation to someone who had never heard the gospel, how would you put it into words?

   _____

   _____

   _____

"God became grace personified when He decided to reach down and extend His love and affection to us" (p. 154).

He made Him who knew no sin to be sin on our behalf, so that we might become the righteousness of God in Him. 2 Corinthians 5:21

5. Read 2 Corinthians 5:21, and describe the "exchange" mentioned in this verse. What comes to mind as you think about this exchange?

   _____

   _____

   _____

6. Read 2 Corinthians 12:9–10. How does God transform our weakness into strength? What are your weaknesses through which Christ can display His strength?

   _____

   _____

   _____

"His greatness and power reveal that you are feeble, insignificant, and weak. This is exactly where He wants us to be, for it is in weakness that His power makes us strong" (p. 154).

7. Take some time to reflect on what God's Word says about how God made a way for us to become jewels in His crown. Review verses we've studied as well as any others you wish to include here.

_____

_____

_____

$\mathcal{A}$PPLYING GOD'S TRUTH

8. After spending time thinking about and studying God's grace, the most appropriate response is some serious praise! If you feel like singing, sing! If you feel like crying out, cry! Capture your enthusiasm and praise in a prayer of thanks to God.

_____

_____

_____

9. Second Corinthians 6:1 cautions us not to receive the gift of God's grace in vain. In what ways have you overlooked or set aside the wonder of God's grace in your life? Confess this to God, and recommit yourself to a renewed awareness and appreciation of His gift of grace to you.

_____

_____

_____

$\mathcal{R}$ECORDING KEY INSIGHTS

10. What verses or insights from today's study were particularly significant to you? Write them below and journal about what they mean to you.

_____

_____

_____

And He has said to me, "My grace is sufficient for you, for power is perfected in weakness." Most gladly, therefore, I will rather boast about my weaknesses, so that the power of Christ may dwell in me. Therefore I am well content with weaknesses, with insults, with distresses, with persecutions, with difficulties, for Christ's sake; for when I am weak, then I am strong. 2 Corinthians 12:9–10

Taking Action

11. What will you do differently as a result of today's study?

_____

_____

_____

SETTING THE STONE

Allow these verses to inspire your prayerful response to God today:

☐ **Romans 5:20–21**—That I will understand grace covers *all* my sin.

☐ **2 Timothy 1:9**—For me to remember the high calling that accompanies my salvation by grace.

☐ **1 John 2:1–2**—That whenever I sin, I will realize Jesus is my faithful Advocate.

Journal notes

Journal notes

PART 29

AND SO MUCH MORE

Refer to chapter 9 in *A Jewel in His Crown*.

*G*EM OF THE DAY

*"Just when we think He's done all He can possibly do for us,
He does a little more" (p. 154).*

1. When have you felt as if what you had done was too much for God to forgive?

_____

_____

*For sin shall not
be master over
you, for you are
not under law
but under grace.
Romans 6:14*

*U*NDERSTANDING GOD'S WORD

2. Salvation is not the end of grace; it is just the beginning. Grace for our daily living—that's the topic of our study. Read 2 Peter 3:18. What does this mean?

_____

_____

_____

*"Some people think of grace only as the path along which we are ushered into salvation.
. . . But too often our thoughts about grace stop there. If so, we have missed out on the
true splendor of our great God's limitless grace" (p. 154).*

3. Grace has changed everything about us. For the believer, every day is a new day! What does Romans 6:14–18 tell us about this truth? As you think about your life right now, would you describe yourself as a slave to sin or a slave to righteousness?

_____

_____

_____

4. Grace is supposed to make a difference in our lives every day. The Bible cautions us not to let God's grace go to waste. Read and then summarize the following verses.

1 Corinthians 15:10 _____

Hebrews 12:15 _____

"What can we do but thank Him? How can we refuse His gift of grace?" (p. 158).

But by the grace of God I am what I am, and His grace toward me did not prove vain; but I labored even more than all of them, yet not I, but the grace of God with me. 1 Corinthians 15:10

5. Read Ephesians 4:7–13. What truths about God's grace do you find in these verses?

_____

_____

_____

"God does not pass out His grace in prepackaged bundles to all who need it, but rather He has tailored His grace just for you" (p. 155).

6. Read 1 Peter 4:10. God expects for us to be good "stewards" of the gifts he has given us by His grace. What gifts have you been given to use for his glory?

_____

_____

_____

7. Take some time to reflect on what God's Word says about grace-filled living. Review verses we've studied as well as any others you wish to include here.

_____

_____

_____

*A*PPLYING GOD'S TRUTH

8.   In what specific situation do you need God's "tailor-made" grace in order to be victorious? Spend some time in quiet reflection, then write out your request to God.

_____

_____

_____

9.   In light of what you've studied in God's Word, how has God's grace affected your past, your present, and your future?

_____

_____

_____

*R*ECORDING KEY INSIGHTS

10.   What verses or insights from today's study were particularly significant to you? Write them below and journal about what they mean to you.

_____

_____

_____

*T*AKING ACTION

11.   What will you do differently as a result of today's study?

_____

_____

_____

And He gave some as apostles, and some as prophets, and some as evangelists, and some as pastors and teachers, for the equipping of the saints for the work of service, to the building up of the body of Christ; until we all attain to the unity of the faith, and of the knowledge of the Son of God, to a mature man, to the measure of the stature which belongs to the fullness of Christ.
Ephesians 4:11–13

SETTING THE STONE

Allow these verses to inspire your prayerful response to God today:

☐ *John 1:16*—That I will experience the fullness of His grace.

☐ *Acts 4:33*—For His grace to empower me to testify of Him.

☐ *Romans 12:6*—That I will use the gifts of grace God has provided to me.

Journal notes

Journal notes

JEWELS FOR HIS GLORY

Refer to chapter 9 in *A Jewel in His Crown*.

*G*EM OF THE DAY

"He has summoned us to be women of excellence" (p. 158).

1. Thoughtfully consider your life's mission. What is most important to you? What is
    your ultimate purpose for living?

    _____

    _____

    _____

*U*NDERSTANDING GOD'S WORD

2. We know that God desires for us to be jewels in His crown. We understand that He is
    able to do so. But why? Why does He want jewels in His crown? Describe the "big pic-
    ture" regarding our royal role in 1 Peter 2:9–10.

    _____

    _____

    _____

3. God wants us to proclaim His excellencies to all the world! We shine and sparkle in praise of His glory! Combined with all the other sparkling jewels in His crown, we honor Him with our radiance. What does Romans 8:17 teach about sharing in His glory?

_____

_____

_____

The twenty-four elders will fall down before Him who sits on the throne, and will worship Him who lives forever and ever, and will cast their crowns before the throne, saying, "Worthy are You, our Lord and our God, to receive glory and honor and power; for You created all things, and because of Your will they existed, and were created." Revelation 4:10–11

"By grace, Jesus Christ has invited us into His royal court. He has offered to dress us in the finest garments. He has called us to share His glory" (p. 158).

4. God enjoys transforming us into a brilliant jewel for our benefit. Ultimately, however, our brilliance is not about *us*. He creates jewels in His crown to magnify *His* name. Read Revelation 4:9–11 and describe what we'll do with our own crowns someday.

_____

_____

_____

5. A woman in the King's court is aware she is in the presence of a holy and awesome God who is worthy of her praise. What does God's Word teach us about His holiness?

Psalm 22:3 _____

Psalm 99:9 _____

Isaiah 57:15 _____

Revelation 4:8 _____

6. Read 2 Thessalonians 1:11–12. What areas of your life are not currently giving God the glory He deserves?

_____

_____

_____

7. You see, the more we realize our royal identity, the more our attitudes and actions will reflect His glory. Read John 15:5–8, and describe how we bring Jesus glory.

_____

_____

_____

8. Take some time to reflect on what God's Word says about living for His glory. Review verses we've studied as well as any others you wish to include here.

_____

_____

_____

$\mathcal{A}$PPLYING GOD'S TRUTH

9. In light of what you have studied, how can you take away from the glory God deserves if you neglect to live as a jewel in His crown? In what ways are you slighting His rightful share of praise by cheapening yourself or rebelling in sin?

_____

_____

_____

My Father is glorified by this, that you bear much fruit, and so prove to be My disciples.
John 15:8

10. Tell God about your intentions to start glorifying Him in every aspect of your life, beginning today, so that every brilliant ray coming from you will illuminate His glory.

_____

_____

_____

RECORDING KEY INSIGHTS

11. What verses or insights from today's study were particularly significant to you? Write them below and journal about what they mean to you.

_____

_____

_____

TAKING ACTION

12. What will you do differently as a result of today's study?

_____

_____

_____

SETTING THE STONE

Allow these verses to inspire your prayerful response to God today:

☐ *Psalm 1:3*—That I will yield fruit and prosper in everything I do.

☐ *Galatians 5:22–23*—That the world will see the fruit of the Spirit in my life.

☐ *Ephesians 1:5–6*—That I will live to the praise of His glory.

☐ *Revelation 5:13*—That I will not wait until heaven to give God the glory due His name.

Journal notes

Journal notes

SINCE 1894, Moody Publishers has been dedicated to equip and motivate people to advance the cause of Christ by publishing evangelical Christian literature and other media for all ages, around the world. Because we are a ministry of the Moody Bible Institute of Chicago, a portion of the proceeds from the sale of this book go to train the next generation of Christian leaders.

If we may serve you in any way in your spiritual journey toward understanding Christ and the Christian life, please contact us at www.moodypublishers.com.

"All Scripture is God-breathed and is useful for teaching, rebuking, correcting and training in righteousness, so that the man of God may be thoroughly equipped for every good work."

—2 TIMOTHY 3:16, 17

MOODY
PUBLISHERS
THE NAME YOU CAN TRUST®

A Jewel In His Crown
Rediscovering Your Value As a Woman of Excellence

ISBN: 0-8024-4083-5

When they become weary and discouraged, women lose sight of their real value as beloved daughters of God. *A Jewel in His Crown* examines how the way women view their worth deeply affects their relationships. This book teaches women how to renew strength and be women of excellence.

Priscilla Shirer herself is a crown jewel, mined from a family of precious gems. Reading her book is like a walk through Tiffany's as she uses her insight to draw the readers attention to the various facets of a godly woman's character. My prayer is that God will use A Jewel in His Crown *to help women embrace their primary aim of brining glory to God through the uniqueness of who they are in Christ.*
  Anne Graham Lotz, AnGel Ministries

MOODY
PUBLISHERS

THE NAME YOU CAN TRUST.

1-800-678-6928 www.MoodyPublishers.com

A Jewel in His Crown Journal Team

Acquiring Editor:
Elsa Mazon

Copy Editor, Interior and Cover Copy:
Livingstone Corporation

Cover Design:
Ragont Design

Printing and Binding:
Versa Press Inc.

The typeface for the text of this book is
Garamond Condensed